The Beginning of the World

The Beginning of the World

Henry M. Morris

Master Books

Please visit our website for other great titles:
www.masterbooks.net

For information regarding publicity for author interviews contact Dianna Fletcher at (870) 438-5288.

Contents

Introduction

The modern creationist movement has not only enlisted thousands of scientists in its ranks, but has been like a breath of fresh air to Bible-believing pastors and Christians generally. Creation-evolution debates have been held on hundreds of university campuses in recent years, and thousands of students have seen and heard firsthand that the entire evolutionary system is scientifically indefensible. "This is the Lord's doing; it is marvelous in our eyes" (Psalm 118:23).

The last three decades have seen a remarkable revival of confidence in the scientific integrity and accuracy of the Scriptures. The neo-orthodox and neo-evangelical movements of the past generation, promoting the idea that the Bible was only a book of "religion," rather than one of science, have proved sterile and self-defeating. Most young people were too intelligent to have assurance for very long in the spiritual teachings of a book that was full of scientific and historical mis-information. If the biblical cosmogony was not acceptable to the modern mind, there was no reason to think that biblical commandments were applicable to modern morality or that the biblical eschatology was meaningful in planning for the future. An introspective emphasis on personal regeneration and "confident living" might satisfy some people for a little while, but such purely emotional religion will not stand the fires of intellectual attack and ridicule very long unless undergirded by solid and intelligent knowledge of the *complete* integrity of God's Word.

While many Christians were compromising the Scriptures with what they thought was modern science, however, God was calling many scientists to the defense of the faith, and the result has been a sudden surge of awareness that the Bible was true after all, even on such long-ridiculed doctrines as a literal six-day creation, a young earth, and a worldwide cataclysmic flood in the days of Noah.

This exciting development has stirred up great new interest in the study of the Book of Genesis. The "Back-to-Genesis" seminars of the Institute for Creation Research, for example, in recent years normally attract well over a thousand registrants each. Especially the first 11 chapters of Genesis, so long explained away even by many evangelicals as allegorical rather than historical, are now being recognized as the very foundation of all history. These marvelous writings, recording the creation, the Fall, the Curse, the flood, and the dispersion, are absolute prerequisites to any comprehension of God's purposes for the world and for individual people in subsequent ages. That is why God placed them first in His Word; they are foundational for all that follows.

There has, however, been a need for a Sunday school quarterly or similar publication that could be used either in classes or for individual study, providing more systematic and detailed analysis of these key chapters of Scripture than can be covered in one seminar of Bible conference. Such a study should be on a layman's level, yet sound and insightful, both biblically and scientifically. That is the goal of the present book.

Although it is published in quarterly format, it provides considerably more substantive content than a typical Sunday school quarterly. Questions for further class discussion, if desired, are appended to each chapter. Users are assumed to be of college age or older, but it should be easily understandable by almost any reader. It should be used by both student and teacher, but the latter also may wish to follow up with the books listed in the appendix as well.

There is a real need for a "back-to-Genesis" emphasis in today's Christian world, and we trust this study book will help fulfill that need.

Chapter 1

A Created Beginning

Genesis 1:1–2

The book of Genesis (meaning "beginnings") is often regarded in these cynical days as nothing but a collection of old legends from earlier less sophisticated times. Some think of the Genesis stories as allegories with certain moral and spiritual values, though not true in a historical sense.

But no one who believes the Bible can accept such ideas. For such a person, Genesis is the foundation upon which the entire edifice of the Bible is built. The New Testament, for example, directly quotes or alludes to the book of Genesis no less than 200 times, with half of these referring to the first eleven chapters of Genesis alone. Jesus Christ Himself quoted or referred to each of the first seven chapters of Genesis. All of these references are of such form as to show that both Christ and the Apostles accepted Genesis not only as fully historical but also as divinely inspired.

The book of Genesis receives its name from the title employed by the translators of the Septuagint (Greek translation of the Hebrew Old Testament). Genesis (Greek: *genesis*) refers to beginnings or origins. Genesis is the book of beginnings or the book of origins.

As we consider the first eleven chapters of Genesis, we shall see that all true scientific and historical data support the truth of the Bible record. And we shall also see that the purposes of God in His great plan of salvation are inseparably bound to these same events. Furthermore, the origin of all basic human institutions (home, family, agriculture, technology, government, etc.) can be found in the book of Genesis.

The Meaning of Creation

In this chapter, we want to consider the cosmic implications of the first two verses of the Bible. These are almost certainly the most widely read words in all literature. (After all, the Bible has for centuries been the world's best seller, and most Bible owners at least *begin* to read the Bible!), and there is a strong probability that they were the *first* words ever written.

The first verse of the Bible is the most important and basic of all. "In the beginning God created the heaven and the earth." When one *really* believes this verse, he will have little difficulty believing all the rest of God's Word. This single verse refutes all the various false theories about origins that men have invented.

The verse refutes atheism ("the doctrine of no God") because it starts with God. Pantheism ("all God") is refuted because it shows that God existed before the universe. Polytheism ("many gods") is false because the universe which was created was not a "poly-verse" and it was created by one God. Dualism, the doctrine of two eternal gods, one good and one evil, is merely a special form of polytheism. Evolutionism is rejected because it says that God *created.*

Actually, all these false philosophies are essentially the same. All theories of origins — other than the true account in the Bible — teach that the present "cosmos" came into existence by the operation of the "gods" or the forces of nature or some mystical principle acting upon the previously existing material "stuff" of the earlier "chaos." This idea is no less prevalent in ancient paganism than in modern scientism. The revelation of the special creation of all things by an eternal and almighty personal God is essentially unique to the Bible! Thus all other explanations of origins, whether religious or philosophical or scientific, are basically only different forms of the concept of evolution.

"Creation" is defined simply as *the work of God in bringing all things into existence.* Only God is eternal — everything else in the universe had a beginning. True creation is creation *ex nihilo* (out of nothing), and is not merely a reworking of materials already in existence.

Opposed to the doctrine of creation is the concept of evolution. Evolution is defined, in its broadest sense, as the theory that all things have been derived by gradual modification through natural processes from previous materials. According to this concept, all forms of life have developed from earlier, simpler forms, and even life itself spontaneously came into existence through a complex organization of previously non-living chemical molecules. Even the basic molecular and atomic structure of matter supposedly developed from still simpler and more basic forms of matter. The theory of evolution, in essentially the above form, is strongly championed by many modern scientists. In fact, the claim is often heard that *all* scientists accept evolution, but this claim is, of course, untrue. There are many scientists and other well educated people today who reject evolution and who insist that only divine creation can account for the universe and its inhabitants.

The key question is whether all things were specially created by the God of the Bible or whether they have developed from prior materials into their present forms through the operation of innate principles. If the latter is true, it follows that this development, this "evolution," is still going on, since presumably the same principles are still in operation.

There are some who suggest that evolution was God's method of creation. However this belief, which is called *theistic evolution,* is not generally accepted either by the real leaders of evolutionary thought or by those who firmly believe in the plenary verbal inspiration and infallibility of Scripture. As a matter of fact, the decision between creation and evolution is not really a scientific decision at all. *Science,* as such, can say nothing whatever about origins. Science (knowledge) is limited to the study of physical phenomena and processes as they exist at present. The scientific method involves reproducibility. That is, an experiment performed today which yields certain results will, if repeated next year, still yield the same results. It must be seen, however, that pre-historic events are not subject to scientific experimentation and therefore no one can say *scientifically* what happened millions of years ago. In order to project our knowledge of *present* processes into the pre-historic past, we must necessarily make certain assumptions as to the basis of such projections. And this involves a philosophy or a faith, not science.

It is significant that *present* processes, which are the only kinds of processes which can be tested by the scientific method, are not in any way *creative* processes. That is, the basic laws of modern science, which describe these present processes, are laws of conservation and deterioration, not of creation and integration. These laws deal with the fundamental behavior of matter and energy, which actually include everything in the physical universe, and are known as the first and second laws of thermodynamics.

Thermodynamics (from two Greek words meaning "heat power") is the science dealing with the conversion of heat and other forms of energy into work. It is now known that everything in the universe is energy in some form, and everything that "happens" is basically an energy conversion process. Thus, the first and second laws of thermodynamics could just as well be called the first and second laws of science. All processes in the universe, as far as known, have to obey these two laws.

The first law of thermodynamics is also called the law of energy conservation. This law states that, although energy can be changed in form, it is not now being either created or destroyed. Since all physical phenomena, including matter itself, are merely different forms of energy, this clearly implies that creation was an event of the past and is no longer going on.

The second law of thermodynamics, stated in nontechnical form, says that all physical systems, if left to themselves, tend to become disorganized. Thus, machines wear out, processes run down, organisms get old and die. Any temporary increase in organization requires an input of energy from outside the system itself.

These two universal laws are basic in all disciplines of modern science. Verified by thousands of experiments, from the nuclear level to the astronomic level, with no known exceptions, they clearly indicate that nothing is *now* being created and that the original creation is "running down."

This all proves, *as well as "science" is able to demonstrate anything,* that evolution, which requires a continuing universal process of development and integration, is simply not true at the present time. This is why no one has seen evolution occurring.

Since "science" can only deal legitimately with *present* processes, and since present processes are not creative or integrative in nature, science as such can tell us nothing about origins. Therefore, if we are to know anything about the Creation — when it was, what methods were used, what order of events occurred, or anything else — we must depend *completely* on divine revelation. There is no other valid source of information on this subject.

God was there and we were not! And He *has* told us quite plainly what took place then, in His revealed Word. The Bible clearly confirms the implications of the two laws of thermodynamics. Such passages as Genesis 2:1–3; Hebrews 4:3,10; Exodus 20:11 and others indicate clearly that the creation was *complete* at the end of the six days of creation. Hebrews

1:10–12; Romans 8:20–22 and similar verses teach that the originally perfect creation is now in a process of decay.

The first two verses of Genesis speak of the initial act of creation of our present physical universe. "In the beginning" speaks of the point at which Time, as we understand it, began. "The heavens" refer to the vast expanses of Space in the universe and "the earth" to the Matter which would occupy Space and Time.

Initially, there were no other stars or planets; these were all made only on the fourth day of the creation week, according to Genesis 1:14 – 19. The "heavens," therefore, were not the stars, but the vast reaches of space in which the stars would later be placed. Even the earth was not initially in the spherical form it now possesses; it was "without form." Nevertheless, the physical universe, which had no existence previously, had come into existence, and Time had begun.

God "created" all these — Time Space and Matter — by His own Word (note Psalm 33:6,9; John 1:1–3; Hebrews 11:3; II Peter 3:5). The verb "create" translates a Hebrew word, *bara,* which is never used with any other subject but God. In other words, only God Himself is able to "create" anything.

The first verse, incidentally, is not a dependent clause (i.e. "in the beginning, when God was creating...the earth was without form..."), as some have maintained. Neither is it a mere title or summary of the chapter. Instead, it is an independent statement describing the first event in the creative work of the first day. This interpretation is required because otherwise there would be no reference in the entire account to the actual creation of "the heavens" as required by Genesis 2:1 and Exodus 20:11.

This fact is also emphasized by the use of the Hebrew conjunction (translated "and") at the beginning of verse 2. This same connective appears at the beginning of each later verse in the chapter, indicating continuous, sequential action throughout the week, one verse after another.

Thus both Scripture and science teach that creation is not now taking place. We are therefore completely unable to study experimentally any of the processes of creation. We must learn whatever we wish to know about it from the only one who can tell us — God Himself. We must approach the Biblical record of creation with an open mind and heart to see and believe what God has said, not with the idea of trying to make it harmonize with some human theory of origins.

It should be remembered that the various popular cosmogonies (a "cosmogony" is a model for explaining the origin of the cosmos), such as the so-called "big-bang" and "steady-state" theories, are strictly man-made evolutionary systems trying to explain the universe without God. It is obvious that such theories are completely outside the realm of science. The essence of science is observation and experimentation, but these are impossible in the study of origins. How can one study, *experimentally,* the origin of a universe or the development of a galaxy?

There is nothing whatever in science to prevent us from accepting the revealed fact that God *created* all things, calling them into existence *ex nihilo* (or, perhaps better, *ex deo*), in a fully developed and functioning state right from the beginning.

This fact is confirmed not only by Scripture but also by the two laws of thermodynamics. The second law states, in effect, that the universe must have had a beginning; otherwise, since it is now running down, it would already be dead. The first law, on the other hand, states in effect that the universe could not have created itself. It must have been created, therefore, by some adequate Cause beyond itself. "In the beginning God created the heaven and the earth" is the most scientific statement that could possibly be made about the origin of the universe, based on the known laws of science.

The second verse describes the initial aspect of the created earth. The verse is correctly rendered "was," and does not need to be rendered "became" as some have contended. It is the regular Hebrew verb of being. Although in some contexts it is legitimately translated "became," this is valid in only about 25 of its more than 1500 occurrences. Obviously the earth at this stage was not "perfect" in the sense that it was complete, until it *was* complete, at the end of the six days, but it was perfect for God's immediate purpose.

The so-called "gap theory," which suggests a tremendous gap of time between Genesis 1:1 and 1:2, is incorrect, being both unwarranted Biblically and impossible scientifically. Exodus 20:11, in the ten commandments, states that "in six days, the Lord made heaven and earth, the sea, and *all that in them is*." Thus, nothing in the earth or sea could have been made *before* the six days. The gap theory is supposed by its advocates to provide time for the geological ages, which were then terminated by a great cataclysm, leaving the earth "without form and void," as described in Genesis 1:2. However, the geological ages are based on the principle of "uniformitarianism," which precludes any such thing as a world-wide cataclysm. Any cataclysm which would leave the earth covered with water and the water shrouded in darkness would have literally destroyed any previous structures in the earth's crust. But the fossils in the sedimentary rocks of the earth's crust provide the only real evidence for the geological ages. The gap theory thus negates itself, trying to accommodate the geological ages by a cataclysm which would destroy the evidence for the geological ages! Genesis 1:2 does not describe the earth after long ages and a great cataclysm, but rather at the very beginning of its history.

Initially the earth's matter was "without form," referring to the fact that waters covered it and possibly contained most of its other substances in solution or suspension. It was also "void" or empty, with no living inhabitants. However, as Isaiah noted over 3000 years afterwards, God had not created the earth "in vain," to be forever "empty," but rather "formed it to be inhabited" (Isaiah 45:18). Thus, He first proceeded to "form" that which was "without form," then to provide inhabitants for that which was "void."

This He did through His Spirit, who *moved* (lit. "was vibrating") in the primeval darkness which surrounded the waters. Through Him, by His Word, would soon flow the boundless power which would bring light out of darkness, lands from the formless waters and living inhabitants from the silent earth.

The God of Creation

God's energizing presence testified of His approval of the work thus far. The "Spirit of God was moving upon the face of the waters." This speaks of the Holy Spirit, whose outflowing power, proceeding from the Father through the Son, is the source of all God's mighty work of creation. There is an interesting parallel between this verse and II Peter 1:20 where we are told that "holy men of God were moved by the Holy Spirit," in the writing of Scripture. The "moving" of the Holy Spirit is thus basic in God's revelation in both nature and the written Word.

It is of supreme importance that we believe in the true God of the Bible. Men have invented many "gods," and Satan is engaged in an age-long attempt to make himself the ruler or "god" of the universe. But there is only one *true* God, and He is the one who has created all things. It is *only* in the Bible that we learn of His nature and character and purposes.

The doctrine of God as taught in Scripture reveals Him to be the triune God. He is Father, Son, and Holy Spirit. The plurality of the Godhead is intimated by the word "God" in the first verse of the Bible, which is the plural form *elohim*.

It is significant that each of the three persons of the Godhead is associated with the work of creation. All good and perfect gifts, which certainly are included in God's "very good" creation, come from the Father, according to James 1:17. The work of the Spirit is clearly stated in Genesis 1:2. But most emphatically the Son is said to be the Word of God by whom the creation was spoken into being. Note such Scriptures as John 1:1–3; Hebrews 1:3; Psalm 33:6; Revelation 3:14, and especially Colossians 1:16, 17. Men need to realize fully that Jesus Christ is God and that it was by Him that all things were created.

The Bible does not try to prove that God exists before telling what He has done. It simply starts with God, taking for granted the fact of His existence and His omnipotence. In fact, Scripture says only a "fool" can say in his heart there is no God (Psalm 14:1). Surely with the evidence all around us of "creation," any truly reasonable man should recognize that there is a "Creator."

The very fact of "intelligible" phenomena of nature in the world should indicate an "intelligence" that caused them. The fact of individual personalities in the world capable of emotions and of the exercise of their wills should indicate a great Person, who exercises love, anger, and His will, as their cause. The fact that all people have an inborn sense that "right" is better than "wrong" testifies that the cause of such instinctive conscience must be a *holy* Creator. The scientific law of cause and effect — that no effect can be greater than its cause — surely applies to these conclusions as well as to those in any other categories of science and logic.

Nevertheless, many men attempt to sidestep such reasoning and still refuse to accept God as He is according to Scripture. They do not "like to retain God in their knowledge," and therefore, "professing themselves to be wise, they become fools" (Romans 1:28, 22).

It is profoundly meaningful that Genesis 1:1 suggests that God is both One and yet more than one. The Hebrew word "God" is *Elohim,* a plural form with the fundamental meaning of "gods" or "the mighty ones." Yet the verb form "created" appears in the singular, requiring a singular subject.

The doctrine of the Trinity is not explicitly formulated in these first two verses, but it is clearly consistent with them. The New Testament speaks of God as Father, Son and Holy Spirit, each distinct and yet each equally and eternally the One God of creation. The Father is the eternal source of all things; the Son as the incarnate Word, reveals the Father; the Spirit proceeds from the Father through the Son, to make applicable and effectual the will of God in His creation.

Thus, the Spirit was "moving" in creation. Motion implies energy, resulting in the various physical phenomena of the creation. This is the essence of what scientists mean by Matter, the phenomena associated with which always involve motion, through Space, in Time. The universe created is thus a Space-Matter-Time "continuum." Space is the ever-present background, within which everywhere occur material phenomena — Matter — the manifestation and application of which everywhere involve Time. Thus, the created physical universe is really a tri-universe, perhaps reflecting the nature of its triune Creator.

In remarkably analogous fashion, these three universal components of creation — Space, Matter, and Time — each exhibit the characteristics of tri-unity. Thus Space is three-dimensional, with each dimension occupying the whole of space and yet all three required for its full reality. Matter finds its unseen but omnipresent source in energy, manifesting itself in some form of motion, resulting in the various phenomena of light, heat, sound, inertia, etc. Energy, then motion, then phenomena — the source, the substance, the result. Likewise, Time is future, present and past, each the whole of time yet each clearly distinct in meaning.

The physical creation thus marvelously appears to be a trinity of trinities! Although this does not *prove* that God is a triune God, it is surely wonderfully consistent with that revealed fact, reflecting throughout all the universe the nature of its Creator. How supremely important it is to know God *as He is,* through

Jesus Christ, "for in Him dwelleth all the fullness of the Godhead bodily" (Colossians 2:9).

Genesis 1:1 clearly states the fact of creation, but this immediately raises the question: Why? God is omniscient and omnipotent, and He therefore must have had a purpose and that purpose must be fulfilled.

As a matter of fact, all the rest of Scripture is occupied with that purpose and its accomplishment. It might be summarized by saying He created the universe for man, and man for Himself.

We trust that the reader is willing to believe fully in God as He is revealed in Scripture. This of course means believing in Jesus Christ as both Creator and Saviour — the One who created all men and who also died to redeem men (John 1:11–13; 3:36; 5:24).

Questions for Discussion

1. In what ways is the Genesis record of the creation of the universe of space, time and matter different from all other cosmogonies?

2. What are the Biblical and scientific arguments for and against the "gap theory"? Why do geologists reject this theory?

3. Define carefully the Biblical doctrine of the trinity, explaining the distinctive roles of the Father, Son and Holy Spirit in the Godhead.

4. Why is theistic evolution incompatible with the nature of God?

5. Explain how the first and second laws of thermodynamics point to the existence of a transcendent Creator of the universe.

6. How does the law of cause-and-effect indicate the existence of a personal (rather than impersonal) God?

7. What significance is implied by the three acts of special "creation" in Genesis 1, as distinct from acts of "making" or "forming"?

Chapter 2

The Six Days of Creation

Genesis 1:3–2:3

In the first chapter, we examined at some length the first two verses of the Bible, learning that the eternal, transcendent, personal God at some finite time in the past called the universe into existence *ex nihilo.* In the beginning, it was merely the basic space-matter-time cosmos in elemental form, static and dark, until the Holy Spirit began to "move" (literally, "hover" or "vibrate") in the presence of the watery matrix in which the elemental earth was originally suspended. Then the cosmos began to be formed and energized. Genesis 1:3–2:3, which we shall examine in this chapter, lists the detailed formative and energizing works of God during the six days of the great "Creation Week."

Events of the Creation Period
(Genesis 1:3–30)

The events of the six days took place before there were any human beings to observe and record them. They would have to be *revealed* by God, either to Moses or, more likely, originally to Adam himself.

After the initial creation "from nothing" of space, time and matter, God proceeded to bring form to the shapeless earth, initially blanketed in water and darkness, and then inhabitants to its silent surface.

First, "God commanded the light to shine out of darkness," even as now He is able to shine into our darkened hearts with the light of His Word, "to give the light of the knowledge of the glory of God in the face of Jesus Christ" (II Corinthians 4:4). It says then that "God called the light Day" (thus plainly defining what is meant by the word "day" when it is used in this chapter). This ended the work of the first day; "evening" came, then a period of darkness, and then "morning," when another "day" began. Although the source of the light was evidently not yet the sun in its present form, the succession of evenings and mornings indicates that the earth's axial rotation had begun. It should be emphasized that these days of creation were literal *days*. This is the Word of God, and God is surely able to say what He means.

It is significant that God's first creative act, after His initial creation of Time ("the beginning"), Space ("the heaven"), and Matter ("the earth") was that of Light, accomplished by His spoken Word. "And God *said,* Let there be light: and there was light."

Light is the most basic of all forms of energy, intimately related to all other forms of energy. It is well-known also that energy is related to matter by the famous Einstein equation, $e=mc^2$. In this equation, c is the velocity of light, the tremendous speed to which all other types of motion in the physical universe must be referenced. Possibly the Scriptures hint at this when, just before the spoken Word produces light, we are told that God the Holy Spirit was "moving" in the darkness over the formless earth.

Many people, of course, have tried to interpret the word "day" in a non-literal sense, attempting in some way to correlate the days of creation with the "ages" of geology. The "day-age" theory, however, encounters insuperable difficulties, both scientific and Biblical, and must be rejected.

In the ten commandments, there is a very important verse, Exodus 20:11, originally written on stone by the finger of God

Himself (Exodus 31:18): "In six days, the Lord made heaven and earth, the sea, and all that in them is," establishing man's six-day work week on the pattern of God's six days of "creating and making" (Genesis 2:3) all His works. The obvious implication from this parallel reference to God's work days and man's work days is that both are the same — that is, literal days. This conclusion is strengthened by the fact that the Hebrew word for "days" (*yamim* — the plural of *yom,* "day"), which is used over 700 times in the Old Testament, *never* in any other place necessarily means anything but literal "days."

Even when used in the singular, as it is several times in Genesis 1, it normally means a literal day — that is as the period of *light* experienced diurnally as the earth rotates on its axis each 24 hours. It is so defined in verse 5, the first time it is used, where we are told that "God called the light Day." Each creative day is marked off by an "evening," ending the period of light, and the "morning," ending the period of darkness. The words "evening" and "morning" are each used more than a hundred times in the Old Testament, always with the literal meaning. The word "day" (Hebrew *yom*) occasionally is used in the sense of "time" (for example, as we might say, "in the time of King Arthur," or "in the day of King Arthur"), but such a usage is always evident from the context. The word is *never* used to mean a definite "period of time," such as say, the "Elizabethan period" or the "Cambrian period." Furthermore, it never means anything except a literal "day" when combined with a numeral or ordinal as it is at the end of each day's work in Genesis 1 ("the evening and the morning were the *first* day," etc.), although this construction occurs more than a hundred times in the books of Moses alone.

We need therefore to recognize plainly that the Biblical "days" of creation were real days, such as we know them today, and cannot possibly be equated with the "ages" of the so-called historical geology. This should not trouble us scientifically, since we have already seen that *science,* as such, is utterly incapable of really telling us *anything* about creation. Science deals only with present processes, with reproducible experiments, and present processes are *not* processes of creation. We prefer, therefore, simply to let God's Word speak for itself concerning what happened in the creation period.

Of the exact nature of this light, and its source, we are not told. Since God "divided" the light from the darkness, and the cyclic succession of "evenings and mornings" began, it is reasonable to conclude that the diurnal rotation of the earth upon its axis began at this time.

A second act of "division" occurred on the second day, when God "divided the waters which were under the firmament from the waters which were above the firmament" (Genesis 1:7). The waters clearly are the same as the "waters" of verse 2, synonymous also with the "deep" of that verse.

Thus, an unknown but substantial part of the earth's primeval waters were elevated far up into the sky, *above* the "firmament." The Hebrew word for "firmament" could also mean "expanse," or "stretched-out space." In the context here, it must correspond to the atmosphere. This was given the name "heaven" (confirming the intimation that the creation of heaven in verse 1 was equivalent to the creation of space), and was the particular space in which, later, birds were to fly (verse 20).

The "waters above the firmament" must have been in the form of invisible water vapor, extending far into space. They provided a marvelous "canopy" for the earth, shielding it from the deadly radiations coming from outer space and producing a wonderful "greenhouse effect," sustaining a uniformly warm, pleasant climate all around the earth. Being invisible, these water vapors were of course transparent to the light of the heavenly bodies which were to be established on the fourth day.

The "waters under the firmament" still constituted a shoreless ocean, but God's next act was to cause the dry land to rise from the ocean and the ocean to retreat into lower basins forming a network of seas. On the same day, God caused vegetation to cover the dry land, grasses and herbs and trees of all kinds. It is important to recognize that the herbs were already bearing seed and the trees already yielding fruit, as soon as they appeared. This further implies that the "dry land" which had just previously come forth from the waters was already prepared with suitable soils and nutrients for the plants. Everything was created in fully developed, completely functioning form. The whole world thus had an "appearance of age," even though newly created. Creation of apparent age is inherent in the very concept of creation. No deception is involved, as some charge, since God has plainly told us these events of creation. There *would* be deception on God's part, on the other hand, if the earth really were billions of years old, since God has plainly said He created everything in six literal days.

The creation of fruit trees on the third day obviously contradicts the evolutionary theory, which says that all kinds of marine animals, including the fishes, evolved long before fruit trees. It also contradicts evolution by saying that the sun and other heavenly bodies were not placed in the sky until the day ("age"?) after the production of fruit trees on the dry land.

On the fourth day, God made the sun and moon and stars, "to give light upon the earth" (Genesis 1:14–19). The sun and moon were constituted as "light bearers," to serve as light sources for the earth during the day and night, respectively. The light source during the first three days, whatever it may have been, was thus replaced with this permanent arrangement.

In addition to their function as lights, the stars were to serve for "signs and seasons, for days and years." Evidently, the light from the stars was established in trails traversing space simultaneously with the stars themselves, fully functioning from the start.

Modern man, with his uniformitarian presuppositions, has developed many hypotheses about the evolution of galaxies and the solar system. All are speculative and no single theory is generally accepted even by astronomers. There is no real evidence, apart from evolutionary assumptions, that the sun or stars came into existence before the earth. The earth, with its highly diversified and organized chemical structure, not to mention its infinite variety of living things, is immeasurably more complex than are the stars which, for all their size, are relatively simple in form and substance. There is nothing unreasonable at all about the Biblical perspective, which views the earth as the center of interest in the physical universe. The stars in the heavens, no less than the waters and land and plants on earth, were prepared by God with a view to the great history of life and redemption that would soon begin on the earth.

All the materials necessary for animal life — water, air, light, plants, and the chemical materials of the earth — were now available. On the fifth day, God made the fish and birds "after their kinds." It is interesting to note that the first animals created (verse 21) were the "great whales" (or sea-monsters), the largest animals that ever lived. It is difficult to harmonize this with the supposed evolution of all organic life from minute one-celled animals!

It is possible that these "sea monsters" actually were the great marine dinosaurs. The word in the Hebrew original is actually the same word translated "dragons" in later Scriptures.

During the first part of the sixth day, God made all the other animals, classified as "cattle, beasts of the earth, and creeping things." The latter term evidently included insects, as well as land reptiles. All of the various types of living creatures were brought forth "after their kinds," a phrase that is used ten times in this chapter. Each basic "kind" of living creature was thus ordained by God Himself. There is not a "great chain of life," in which all creatures are inter-related by descent, as per the theory of evolution. Undoubtedly, the genetic system of each "kind" was sufficiently complex to permit the later development of many variations within it, but the basic "kind" was fixed by God in the creation.

Note that the order here — land mammals, reptiles, insects — contradicts the evolutionary order, according to which insects evolved long before land mammals and reptiles.

The grand climax of God's creative activity was the making of man, the one who was to have dominion over the earth and all its living creatures. He was also to "subdue" the earth, which warrants his seeking to understand its physical processes (science) and to control them for man's use (technology).

It is significant that plant life was brought forth from the earth (verse 11), implying that its material substance would be of the same elements as in the inanimate earth itself. Similarly, the bodies of animals were formed from the earth and water (verses 20, 24), but they also possessed "souls." The term "creature" of verse 21 is the Hebrew *nephesh*, usually translated "soul." Thus, plants have a living body, but animals have both body and soul.

Man alone has body, soul and spirit! This is revealed by the statement that God created man "in IIis own image." Parenthetically, we might note also here the intimation of the plurality of the Godhead. God said "Let *us* make man in *our* image," but then God created man in *His* own image. It is by his spirit, in communion with God through His Spirit, that man may have fellowship with his Creator, and it is essentially this that sets him apart from all the animals. Man's body is fundamentally no different chemically from either the animate or inanimate creation, though immensely superior in its degree of organization. Similarly, his "soul" — his consciousness, his intelligence, his feelings, his senses — is essentially the same as that of the animal, though again immensely superior in degree of organization.

But man's spirit is unique among all creatures! This is the "image of God."

This "image of God" in man has been marred by man's fall into sin, but not obliterated (see Genesis 9:6; James 3:9). It can even now be restored through faith in Him who is both Son of God and Son of Man, who is perfectly the "image of the invisible God" (Colossians 1:15; Hebrews 1:3). Man's spiritual nature, dead in trespasses and sins, can be renewed by the new birth (John 3:6; Ephesians 4:23, 24; Colossians 3:10).

God's Evaluation of Creation
(Genesis 1:31–2:3)

The creation of man was the climax and conclusion of God's creative acts. Man was to "fill" (not "replenish," which is an incorrect translation of the Hebrew verb) the earth and "subdue" it and to exercise dominion over all other creatures. Because of the Fall and the Curse, this dominion is not now exercised (Hebrews 2:8) except in an incomplete and imperfect fashion. It will one day be restored. The prophecy of Isaiah 11:6–9, anticipating the glories of the millennium, pictures the ideal relations between man and the animal kingdom which must have existed before man's fall.

Chapter 1 of Genesis really should extend through Chapter 2:3, and possibly through the first part of verse 4. In this Epilogue to the creation narrative are revealed two extremely important truths.

In the first place, we are told that "God saw *everything* that He had made, and behold, it was very good." This is the seventh time in the chapter that God pronounced His creative works "good." Thus, any evidences of disorder, of antagonisms, of suffering, of decay, of struggle, and above all, of death, which we now see in the present world or in the records of the past, cannot possibly be attributed to anything occurring during the six days of creation. Something happened *after* creation to bring these into the world. *"By man came death"* (I Corinthians

15:21). Thus fossils of former living creatures, preserved in the rocks of the earth's crust, could not have been buried either before or during the creation period.

In the second place these three verses emphasize over and over again that God's creation was completed. "The heavens and the earth were *finished* ... God *ended* his work ... he *rested* ... in it he *had rested* from *all* his work which God *created and made*."

It should be noted also that there is no ground for sharply distinguishing between God's acts of "creating" and of "making." Thus, He "created" great whales and every living creature (verse 21), but He "made" the beasts and cattle and creeping things (verse 25). Similarly, He "made" man in His own image (verse 26), but He also "created" man in His own image (verse 27). Though the two terms are not precisely synonymous, the emphasis throughout is on the work of God in "creating and making" all things (Genesis 2:3).

The "creative" acts of God were those by which materials and entities which had no prior existence at all were called into being when God "created" them. When God is said to have "made" something, on the other hand, the idea stressed is that He was raising the created material into a higher state of order and organization than it had before. The two terms, when describing acts of God are otherwise essentially synonymous.

In any case, it is plainly stated that everything which God *"created and made"* was completed in the six days. The six days were thus days of both "creating" and "organizing," and the processes which God used then are no longer in operation. The present order of things, which is the only system which science can study experimentally, is one of "conserving" and "disorganizing," as enunciated by the first and second laws of thermodynamics, respectively.

Recognition of the necessity for creation of "apparent age" and of a "finished creation" will go far toward resolving the apparent conflict between the Bible account of creation and the supposed great age of the earth and the universe. Geologic and astronomic dating methods are necessarily based on rates of change in *present* physical processes. The *assumption* is made that the rate and the process have always been the same and that the entity being measured started from a beginning of "zero." This permits a calculation of "apparent age," but ignores the possibility that the apparent age may have been, at least in part, *created!* It also ignores the fact that these rates must conform to the two laws of thermodynamics; in fact, most of the rates used for dating purposes are actually rates of decay. They can therefore tell nothing about the events of creation, which was *completed* by creative processes rather than decay processes. Such calculations also ignore the fact that the assumption of uniformity in process rates is completely invalid in the light of the world-destroying Flood in the days of Noah, which we shall study later.

God's present work (John 5:17) is that of *providence,* "upholding all things by the word of His power" (Hebrews 1:3). These are the processes which scientists can study and which engineers can utilize in their efforts to "subdue the earth." But God's processes of "creating and making" have been terminated, and are thus completely inaccessible to scientific investigation and evaluation. This is confirmed by the law of energy conservation — the most important and certain of all scientific laws — which affirms that nothing is now being either created or annihilated. All so-called scientific theories of origins, if based on extrapolation of present processes, that is, the assumption that present processes are a continuance of creation processes, are bound to be wrong. Only God can tell us the truth about the origin of the universe and its inhabitants, and this is exactly what He has done in this first, incomparable chapter of His Word! Men and women may refuse to believe it, preferring to believe in a naturalistic, humanistic concept of origins. That is *their* problem, and they will have to explain to God someday why they refused to believe the simple, plausible, scientifically reasonable, statements in His Word.

Questions for Discussion

1. What is the probable nature of the Genesis "kind" in relation to the modern "species" concept?

2. List some of the contradictions between the order of events in the Genesis record and the order of evolution in the geological "ages."

3. Why can "day" in Genesis 1 not be translated "geological age"?

4. Discuss the implications of the "waters above the firmament."

5. What is the difference between God's works of "creation" and "providence"?

6. In what sense is God now "resting," yet also now "working"?

7. Discuss the astronomical basis of the day, month and year, in contrast to the lack of such basis for the week. Why is this important?

Chapter 3

Human Origins

Genesis 2:4–17

The Death of Adam is the title of a well-known book on human evolution, a title which emphasizes the widely prevalent opinion among intellectuals that the Genesis account of man's origin has been completely repudiated by modern science. In place of Adam we are told that our ancestors have names like *Pithecanthropus* and *Australopithecus*. Textbooks everywhere proclaim evolution to be a fact of history which all educated people must accept, and this propaganda and pressure are extremely difficult to resist. But when one examines the actual evidence, he sees an amazingly different picture. The Biblical accounts of man's creation has not been discredited at all, but simply rejected! Evolution has not been proved, but simply assumed.

The Facts of Creation

One of the common "proofs" cited by those who reject the doctrine of plenary inspiration of the Bible is that it contains two contradictory accounts of creation. The creation narrative of Genesis 1, which we have studied, is supposed to present a wholly different picture than the "second" creation story in Genesis 2.

But if this is so, it is strange that the Lord Jesus, when answering the Pharisees' question about marriage (Matthew

19:4,5), quoted from both chapters (Genesis 1:27 and 2:24) in the very same sentence! He who was Himself the Creator regarded the records of both chapters as not only harmonious but also as divinely inspired Truth. Rather than leading into contradictions, we shall see that the apparent differences in the accounts give the stronger assurance that the records are true.

The second chapter of Genesis gives information about the creation week which is supplemental, not contradictory, to the outline record of Genesis 1. Genesis 2:1–4a, of course, is really a part of chapter 1, so that the second chapter should begin with the second half of Genesis 2:4. Verses 5 and 6 probably refer to events of the first four days of creation week, and the rest of the chapter to events of the sixth day.

Further information is given about man's original environment, and this is of such detailed character and so different from present conditions as to suggest quite strongly that the account was originally written by an eye-witness. Although the authorship of Genesis has been commonly ascribed to Moses, there is no reason why he should not have incorporated earlier records into the book, and the recurring use of the formula: "These are the generations of ..." indicates that this is a very strong possibility.

It is probable that Moses was here utilizing, as he wrote the book of Genesis, ancient records that had been handed down from the times of the patriarchs whose names were affixed to the respective divisions. At least one of these genealogical histories, that of Adam (Genesis 5:1), was said to have been in a *book*, and therefore in writing, and it is likely that all of them were actual written records.

The word "generations" (Hebrew, *tholedoth*) provides the very name "Genesis" which was first assigned to this book when it was translated into the English. "Genesis" is based on the Greek Septuagint's use of the Greek *genesis* as the equivalent to the Hebrew *tholedoth*. It is the same form that appears in Matthew 1:1: "The book of the generation (Greek, *genesis*) of Jesus Christ." Its basic meaning is "genealogical history" and refers normally to prior, rather than subsequent history.

It is unnecessary to assume that the early histories in Genesis were transmitted orally down to Moses; it is now known that writing was common for at least hundreds of years before Abraham, and there is no reason (other than evolutionary bias) to think that the antediluvians were not literate also. Such a supposition implies that mankind existed for at least 2500 years without any kind of written record or revelation of God's dealings with man.

It may not always be clear whether the phrase, "These are the generations of ..." is placed at the beginning or ending, or in the middle of the record associated with it. Reasons for taking it as a subscript (or ending) in these studies are the following: (1) the first occurrence, Genesis 2:4, necessarily must apply to the narrative preceding it; (2) the individual named could in every case have had access to information concerning events preceding, but not those following, the statement; (3) the use of such a subscript was common literary practice in the ancient tablets. For a scholarly and convincing presentation of these and other related evidences, see *New Discoveries in Babylonia about Genesis,* by P. J. Wiseman.

In each case it will be noted that the individual so named (Adam, Noah, Sons of Noah, Shem, etc.) could have had access to the information contained *before* his name but not that in the division *following* it. Throughout the entire book, the many intimate details and descriptions indicate that the accounts must originally have come from eye-witnesses. It is significant too, that although Moses is referred to 80 times in the New Testament, and the book of Genesis is quoted or referred to 200 times, nowhere is the statement ever made that Moses was the author of any specific quotation from Genesis.

The original "generations" (or "genealogical histories") were thus quite possibly written by the ancient patriarchs themselves, very probably on tablets of stone or clay. Moses, guided by the Holy Spirit, then compiled and organized them into a continuous narrative with appropriate additions of his own, retaining the signatures of each of the original writers to identify the origin of each section. The twelfth and last division, extending from Genesis 37:2 to the end of the book, and telling the story of the twelve sons of Jacob, was then possibly fully written by Moses himself, on the basis of records kept by Jacob's sons and their descendants in Egypt.

The only division without a human signature is the first one, Genesis 1:1–2:4, closed by the statement "These are the generations of the heavens and the earth when they were created." Obviously there was no human witness to record the creation events of this first chapter. God Himself must have given it by direct revelation.

Although we cannot actually prove the foregoing theory of the writing, preserving, and compiling of the book of Genesis, it seems consistent with all the known facts. It is thus quite probable that we have in all essentials the original, eye-witness accounts, written by the very patriarchs themselves!

This, of course, also accounts for the fact that there are differences in style and vocabulary in the different divisions of Genesis, a phenomenon which has, for 200 years been one of the chief bastions of unbelief. The so-called "documentary theory," ascribing a "composite origin" to the books of Moses (the JEDP hypothesis) was based originally on the observation that different names for God were used in the first and second chapters of Genesis. But this is no problem at all when we recognize the probability that the first (Genesis 1:1–2:4) was written directly by God and the second (Genesis 2:4–5:1) by Adam.

In adopting the position that Moses used earlier written records in writing Genesis, we nevertheless recognize that two other views are possible: (1) he could have used earlier verbal records; (2) he could have received the entire narrative by direct revelation. However, neither of these latter methods was employed by God in inspiring the other historical books of the Bible, which were all written either by eye-witnesses or from the direct verbal or written testimonies of eye-witnesses.

Also it is important to note that this "verbal transmission" theory and "vision theory" of Genesis have been often used by doubting scholars to support their denial of the historical and scientific veracity of Genesis 1–11. However, if these chapters were originally written by actual witnesses of the events, guided both in their original writing and also in their later compilation by divine inspiration, then we have the very highest assurance of their absolute accuracy!

We recognize that the so-called higher critics have rejected the Mosaic authorship of the Pentateuch (the first five books of the Bible) and have substituted instead their "documentary hypothesis," also known as the "JEDP" hypothesis. This concept suggests that four or more unknown writers were responsible for various parts of the Pentateuch, all of whom lived many hundreds of years after Moses. These writers were dubbed J, E, D, and P, and their contributions are supposedly identifiable by their different vocabularies and other internal evidences.

This strange theory has been utterly refuted and discredited again and again by conservative Old Testament scholars, but the religious "liberals" who advocate it will nearly always be found unwilling even to read any of the writings of conservative scholars. Thus they still teach it. The idea was based essentially on the following premises: (1) that writing was unknown in Moses' time — a theory that is now known by all archaeologists to be quite ridiculous; (2) that the literary style was later than that of Moses' day — a notion based on ignorance of early literature and since proved false; (3) that the advanced civilization described in Moses' writings was impossible — a charge also founded on ignorance of early civilizations as revealed by more recent archaeological discoveries; (4) that the stories of the Pentateuch must have been based on early legends — a belief which ignores the more reasonable position that the legends of ancient peoples might actually be distorted reflections of the true histories preserved in the ancient records of Genesis; and (5) the evolutionary theory, according to which the Hebrews were a primitive tribe with an evolving religion which eventually developed into the Hebrew theology — a notion which completely begs the question, assuming a universal process of evolution which the writings themselves deny.

Verses 4–6 are difficult to translate. A possible paraphrase is as follows: "In the day that the Lord God made the earth and heavens there was as yet no field plant in the earth and no field shrub growing, since the Lord God had not yet established rainfall on the earth and since there was as yet no man to cultivate the ground. But then there arose water vapors from the earth which watered the whole face of the ground, and the Lord God formed man...."

At first, with no means of getting the necessary water and with no human inhabitants, plants intended for use as cultivated crops were seemingly omitted from the plants caused to start growing on the third day. But these two needs were met when, first, God established the original means of bringing water to the earth (verses 6, 10) and, second, when God made man. He was then ready to *plant* the first garden (verse 8).

It is very likely that there was no rainfall on the earth until after the Flood. The rainbow was an entirely new sign from God to man after the Flood. This could indicate that rain as we know it, as well as the rainbow, were new experiences after the Flood (Genesis 9:11-17).

The record describes man's original environment as most beautiful and congenial. The "waters above the firmament" (Genesis 1:7) seem to have been a vast canopy of invisible water vapor. The "greenhouse effect" of this blanket would have prevented strong temperature differences or rapid temperature changes anywhere on the earth. This in turn would have prevented strong winds and storms. The present hydro-logic cycle, by which waters evaporated from the ocean are moved inland by winds, finally to condense and fall to the earth again, would have been impossible under these conditions. Rather, the waters evaporated daily from the many "seas" (Genesis 1:10) would have moved only short distances from their source before condensing again at night on the adjacent land surfaces (Genesis 2:6).

In addition to many shallow and narrow inter-connected seas, there were evidently rivers fed by artesian springs from a network of subterranean reservoirs and conduits. These reservoirs were the "great deep" which later erupted at the time of the Flood (Genesis 7:11). One of these river systems watered the garden planted by God in Eden (Genesis 2:10–14).

The garden was specially intended for man's home. It must have been wonderfully beautiful and pleasant (*Eden* means "pleasantness"), with the trees bearing a wide variety of delicious fruits. In the very center of the garden was the tree of life. There have been many speculations about this tree and how eating of its fruit might enable one to "live forever" (Genesis 3:22), but we may as well admit we simply do not know what it was. It is also mentioned in Revelation 2:7; 22:2 and 22:14, as being in the new Jerusalem, "in the midst of the Paradise of God," bearing "twelve manner of fruits," with leaves "for the health of the nations."

Neither do we know the physical characteristics of the fruit of the "tree of knowledge of good and evil." God told Adam he could eat freely (literally: "eating, thou mayest eat") of *any* of the trees, except this one. But eating of this tree, he was warned, would result in death (literally: "dying, thou shalt die"). Thus, man would, in the very day of disobedience, enter into a state of "dying," which would lead surely and ultimately to death.

This version of man's origin stresses the earthy origin of his body. There are about fourteen chemical elements which are the chief components of living flesh, among them hydrogen, carbon and oxygen. These are the same as the elements of the earth itself. "The first man is of the earth, earthy" (I Corinthians 15:47).

Then God "breathed into his nostrils the breath of *lives*" (note the plural, which is the correct translation) and man became a "living soul." Man had both the life possessed by plants, permitting the biologic processes of metabolism and reproduction, and the life possessed by animals, involving self-consciousness, intelligence and feelings. It is significant that animals also have "the breath of lives" (Genesis 7:22) and are called "living souls" (Genesis 1:21).

As pointed out before, however, the really unique difference between man and animals is that man was created and made in the image of God (Genesis 1:26, 27).

God planted the beautiful garden for man in the region called Eden. From one part of Eden, the great river gushed forth through the artesian fountain from the great deep, coursing through the garden to provide water for its beautiful trees and shrubs. After leaving the garden, the river parted into four distributaries, eventually emptying into the primeval seas.

There is obviously nothing like this river system or the garden of Eden in the present world. We know that, later, the great Flood completely destroyed the antediluvian world and its geographical features. However, certain place names, such as Ethiopia, Assyria, Euphrates, and others in the early geography were evidently carried over by the occupants of the Ark and given to post-Flood regions and rivers which reminded them of those left behind.

The Fallacies of Evolution

Over against the simple and reasonable Biblical account of the creation of the earth and its inhabitants, we have the concept of organic evolution, which, in its broadest sense, is the theory that all things have been derived by gradual modification through natural processes from previous materials. According to this theory, man and all other living creatures have developed by natural descent from primitive beginnings over hundreds of millions of years of earth history. Life itself is attributed to a fortuitous combination of complex chemicals in some primeval sea. The biologic processes of gene mutations (sudden, hereditary changes in the structure of the germ cell) and natural selection (the response of creatures to their environment such that better-adapted individuals survive and others die out) are supposed to account for the progressive development of all the various types of plant and animal life in the world today. The leaders of evolutionary thought reject the idea that this process is superintended by God. Rather, it is contended that since evolution can explain the world without God or creation, therefore belief in a divine Creator is completely unnecessary and unscientific.

But as we have repeatedly emphasized, true science can deal only with the present; it can tell us nothing about origins. Evolution is not a science; it is a faith — and a very naive and credulous faith at that! Note some of its fallacies, as follows: (1) Evolution supposedly explains the "creation" of all things in terms of *present* processes, but the first law of thermodynamics says that nothing is now being "created." (2) Evolution presupposes an innate tendency towards progress and increasing order and complexity in the universe, but the second law of thermodynamics proves there is an innate tendency towards decay and disorder in the universe. (3) Evolution supposedly is brought about by gene mutations but almost 100 per cent of all known mutations, are harmful or even fatal to the creatures which experience them. (4) No example of true evolution from one basic "kind" into another "kind" is known either in the present world or in the fossil record of the past. (5) Evolutionary kinship of all creatures would imply a continuous intergrading of all forms of life, but both present life and the records of past life show great gaps between all the different kinds of plants and animals. (6) Natural selection supposedly accounts for the development of new kinds, but actually tends to preserve the present kinds, since an incipient organ or new feature of any kind would have no "survival" value unless it were fully functional from its very beginning. (7) Evolution contradicts the scientific law that no effect can be greater than its cause, since it assumes that intelligence was developed from non-intelligent matter, that morality was evolved from non-moral processes, that love and other emotional qualities came out of unfeeling chemicals, that infinitely complex structures arose from simple beginnings, and that spiritual consciousness began out of inert molecules.

The vaunted evidences of evolution are actually quite trivial. Some of them, such as the evidence of comparative anatomy, molecular homology and embryological resemblances, are based on the assumption that similarities in appearance prove evolutionary kinship. But such similarities can be explained much better on the basis of a common Designer, who provided similar structures and mechanisms for similar physiologic functions.

The evidences of variation, hybridization and mutation do, of course, show that biologic *change* is quite common. The genetic system of each "kind" is highly complex, with provision for a tremendous amount of variation. New varieties can thus be formed by the mechanisms of variation, selection and segregation. But such changes are always within the limits fixed by the composition of the genetic material already available, that is, within the limits of the created "kind." *Mutations,* on the other hand, are actual changes in the basic genetic structure, brought about by powerful radiations or chemicals. However, any such random change in a highly organized system can only result in a decrease in organization and viability, in accordance with the second law of thermodynamics. Thus, practically all known mutations are harmful, not helpful, in the struggle for existence.

The only evidence for evolution which is not completely circumstantial is that of the fossil record, which supposedly shows the actual evolutionary progression of life through the ages. However, the fossil record is actually composed mainly of "gaps," with a universal and systematic absence of any intermediate or transitional forms showing how one kind of organism evolved into a higher kind. Furthermore, as we shall see later, there is much evidence that these fossils, instead of representing the evolution of life over many ages, really represent the catastrophic extinction of life in one age. The fossils actually were buried largely in the sediments of the great Flood, and therefore represent the flora and fauna of the antediluvian world.

As far as man's origin is concerned, there is no real evidence of any kind that disproves the Biblical revelation that Adam was the first man, formed by God out of the chemical materials in the earth but also created spiritually in God's own image. All present and past tribes of men (and these include the various prehistoric tribes of "cave-men," and other supposedly "primitive" men) are descended from Adam. Some of these, because of sin, inbreeding, disease or other causes, may even have *degenerated* into an ape-like appearance in some respects (although one should be aware that many of the most-publicized of these "ape-men" are actually based on extremely limited and doubtful fossil evidence). There is certainly no clear-cut series of fossil hominids leading up to man. Even among evolutionary anthropologists there exists today much controversy as to man's true ancestors. Most of the more familiar ape-men — *Pithecanthropus, Sinanthropus, Australopithecus,* and others — are believed by many anthropologists to represent evolutionary "blind alleys," with man's real ancestors still unknown. And this of course is what we should expect — since Adam had no ancestors!

It is significant that a number of fossils of true man have been excavated in recent years from formations dated by the standard methods of geochronometry as *older* than all these so-called evolutionary ancestors of man. Modern evolutionary anthropologists are in great disagreement among themselves as to the actual sequence of human evolution. So far as the real fossil evidence is concerned, there are many fossils of apes and many of men, but no fossil intermediates between apes and men.

But even if, for the sake of argument, we assume that there did exist in the past tribes of men with some simian characteristics, this still would not in any way prove the theory of human evolutionary kinship with the apes. In general, man's body is immensely superior in its degree of organization to that of the animals, but it *is* fundamentally of the same materials. Similarly, his "soul" is basically identical with animal life, though immensely superior in organization. But it is in his *spirit* that man is completely separated from all animals by an impassable gulf.

Only man is able to reason and analyze, to accumulate and transmit knowledge, even from generation to generation. Only man has real language — the ability to communicate in abstract, symbolic speech. Above all, it is only man who can pray and worship God. In spite of widespread evolutionary propaganda in the schools and other institutions of modern society, it should be emphasized that there is not yet any evidence whatever, either scientific or Biblical, for human evolution — or, for that matter, any other type of "vertical" evolution from simple systems into more complex systems. The evidence for special creation of all the real world is abundant and satisfying.

With respect to the often-repeated claim that scientists universally believe in evolution, the reader may be encouraged to know that there are today thousands of qualified scientists who are thorough-going Biblical creationists. For example, the Creation Research Society, organized in 1963, has a membership of over 700 such scientists, each with at least an M.S. degree, representing literally every field of modern science, and each believing in special creation and in the verbal inspiration of the Bible.

There is, therefore, no justifiable reason for anyone to question the complete accuracy of the wonderful account of creation recorded here in the first two chapters of the Bible.

Questions for Discussion

1. Are there any real contradictions between Genesis 1 and Genesis 2? Explain.

2. Discuss the different theories of original authorship of the book of Genesis. Which do you think is best supported Biblically?

3. What is implied by the statement that there was no rain in the world as originally created?

4. How can one harmonize the creation of plants and animals with the theory of organic evolution?

5. What does the Genesis account of the origin of man teach with regard to his relation to God?

6. Critique the evidence of evolution as suggested by the various hominids.

7. Is there a difference between the "soul" and "spirit" in human beings?

Chapter 4

Origin of Home and Family

Genesis 2:18–25

In these last verses of Genesis 2, we come to the climax of God's work of creation. Central in God's plan was the creation of man for fellowship with Himself. But man was to "fill the earth" and exercise "dominion" over it (Genesis 1:28), and this would require provision for "multiplying" and the establishment of human social institutions to carry out this purpose. Of all such institutions, the first and most important was that of the home and family, established by the union of husband and wife. Other human institutions—government, the school, the church—all find their pattern and purpose originally in the basic family unit. Mutual love between husband and wife and between parents and children, with the proper exercise of authority and obedience as directed by God, is thus fundamental to the accomplishment of God's purpose.

The First Marriage (Genesis 2:18–22)

The integrity and permanence of the individual home is thus of such great importance that God made it plain from the beginning that marriage was intended to be permanent until death. It is true, of course, that with marriage as well as with all other human activities, "God hath made man upright; but they have sought out many inventions" (Ecclesiastes 7:29). Polygamy, easy divorce, adultery and other distortions of the marriage covenant have permeated many cultures but, as the

Lord Jesus said. "… from the beginning it was not so" (Matthew 19:8).

The Lord Jesus Himself thus not only confirmed the divine origin of permanent, monogamous marriage (note also Matthew 5:31, 32; Luke 16:18), but also indicated His acceptance of the account of Adam and Eve as the true record of the origin of the human race. It is not surprising, therefore, that a breakdown of the concept of the sacredness of marriage and the home, accompanied by a general decline in morality, has followed the widespread acceptance of the evolutionary philosophy of origins. If man believes he has an animal origin, then why should not he live and behave like other animals!

However, man is *not* related to the animals, as this passage makes very clear. He was to exercise authority *over* them, but he could have no spiritual fellowship *with* them. Only he had been created "in the image of God."

At the end of the sixth day of creation "God saw everything that he had made and, behold, it was *very good*" (Genesis 1:31). But immediately after He made Adam, He said: "It is *not good* that the man should be alone" (Genesis 2:18). God's creation was not finished until a companion and helper could be provided for man.

God first arranged for Adam to become familiar with His other creatures and so brought them to him for naming. This activity may have had two purposes. First, since Adam was to be responsible for exercising dominion over all creatures, it was needful that he should know them and their characteristics. Presumably the name which he assigned to each was in harmony with its appearance or actions. Second and more important, he would recognize in this way that he himself was different from all other living creatures. "There was not found an help meet for him" (literally, "a helper like him") (Genesis 2:20).

There is thus quite clearly no kinship between man and the animals, as the evolutionist would imply. Man is a special creation, with an eternal spirit, and no superficial physiological resemblance to the animals can discredit this.

Whereupon God proceeded to provide the perfect solution for man's loneliness. A woman was formed "of the man" (I Corinthians 11:12). The woman would serve as his helper in carrying out God's plan. She would be his life-companion and the mother of his children. Together they would teach their children about God and His will. Their home would serve as the foundation and pattern for all future families.

Thus was the first marriage to be consummated and the first home established. Although men have often gone far astray from this ideal in later times, it is still true that this is God's pattern for a truly happy and effective home and marriage.

It may be noted here in passing that the supposed discrepancy between this account of the animals and the record of their creation in Genesis 1:20–25 is actually non-existent. It has been claimed that Genesis 2:19 teaches that God made the animals *after* He made man. However, the word "And" at the beginning of this verse can as well be read in the sense of "Also" as in the sense of "Then." Furthermore, the Hebrew verb form in the past tense is the same as for the pluperfect tense, with the context deciding which is correct. Thus the statement should be read as follows: "Also the Lord God had formed out of the ground every beast of the field. ..."

It may be significant that only the "beasts of the field" (probably domestic animals) and the "fowls of the air" are specifically mentioned as named by Adam. Possibly only these were considered to be sufficiently gregarious in nature to be potential companions for man. But even these were not "meet for him." There could be no fellowship of the spirit, since none of the animals had "the image of God."

Having thus shown to Adam his need of a companion and helper like himself, God then undertook His final formative act of the creation week — an act rich in both physical and spiritual meaning. Quite possibly God explained to Adam what

He was going to do — since Adam later seemed to have understood clearly how God had formed Eve.

In any case, God put Adam into a deep sleep and performed a marvelous "surgical operation." The sleep was not necessary to prevent pain, since there was as yet no knowledge of pain or other suffering in the world. There must therefore have been spiritual implications in the "deep sleep." It seems almost as though Adam "died" when as yet there was no death in the world, in order that he might obtain a bride.

From this side of Calvary, the Christian can hardly fail to see here God's first proclamation of the *everlasting* gospel (Revelation 14:6), telling of the One who was "slain from the foundation of the world" (Revelation 13:8). Though Adam may not have known much more, he would forever be impressed with the formation of new life and perfect fellowship out of what appeared, but for God, to be the cessation of life!

It is probable that the word "rib" is a mistranslation. The Hebrew word *tsela* appears 35 times in the Old Testament and this is the only time it has been rendered by "rib." Most of the time (in at least 20 of its occurrences), it means simply "side." Probably the verse should be translated therefore as follows "... and he took one of his sides, and closed up the (remaining) flesh in the stead of (that which he had taken); And the side, which the Lord God had taken from man, made he a woman, and brought her unto the man."

In what sense did the Lord take one of Adam's sides? A "side" would include both flesh and bones, and it is significant that Adam later said: "This is now bone of my bones, and flesh of my flesh."

Although it is not mentioned, it is also obvious that such an operation would release blood through the opened side. In fact, the very "life of the flesh is in the blood" (Leviticus 17:11; Genesis 9:4). Physiologically it is the blood, carrying the necessary oxygen and other chemicals from the air and food taken in by man, that sustains the chemical substance and functions of man's body—both flesh and bones. Possibly it was *only* the blood that God took from Adam's open side, but at least it must have flowed out *with* the flesh and bones.

And again, this immediately reminds us of the One whose side was pierced on Calvary as He was in the "deep sleep" of death, of whose body "not a bone was broken," but from whose side "forthwith came there out blood and water" (John 19: 34–36).

From the "life" of Adam, the blood sustaining his bones and his flesh, God made Eve, his bride. Just so, we who constitute the "bride" of Christ, have received life by His blood (John 6:53–56). So, as the Apostle Paul says: "We are members of his body, of his flesh, and of his bones" (Ephesians 5:30).

Eve was thus made from Adam's side, to work alongside him in carrying out the divine commission to "fill the earth" and to "subdue" it. She not only had the same "flesh" (that is, *body*) and "life" (that is, *soul*) as did Adam, but she also had an eternal *spirit,* as did he, but the spirit was directly from God, not mediated through Adam as was her physical life. This we know from Genesis 1:27: "So God created man in his own image: ... male and female *created* he them." The "image of God," directly created by God was given to both man and woman.

Similarly, although all the descendants of Adam and Eve have inherited their physical and mental characteristics by genetic transmission, yet each individual has a spirit directly from God, and thus is himself capable of personal and eternal fellowship with God. It is God who "formeth the spirit of man within him" (Zechariah 12:1) and to whose disposal each man's spirit "returns" (Ecclesiastes 12:7) when his body returns to dust.

This story is the despair of the so-called "Christian evolutionist." It is utterly impossible to harmonize this account of the origin of woman with any theory of human evolution. This of course is no reason for us to doubt it. As we have seen, the events of creation week were accomplished by God's own powers of "creating and making" — that is, of bringing into existence and then ordering and organizing — all things. These processes are *not* the physical processes of "conservation and disorganizing" which now control the universe and which alone science is able to study. Thus, the only way we can *know* how the world and all things therein were "created and made" is for God to tell us. And in this divinely inspired account, possibly through the record transmitted by Adam himself, we do have the desired information.

The "Christian evolutionists" who say they believe in a *real* Adam, but who also try to accept the evolutionary theory of man's origin, are being inexcusably inconsistent. They say that man's body evolved by evolutionary processes from simian ancestry but then, at the right moment, God created man's spirit and *this* first man was Adam! But then, what about the formation of Eve out of Adam? There is obviously no way that the account of Eve's origin can possibly be harmonized with the evolutionary picture, if words have any meaning at all.

It is significance also that ethnologists and anthropologists find evidence that monogamous, permanent marriage has everywhere and in all ages been considered as the ideal and preferred form of family life. It is unhappily true that often this system has been corrupted; we find divorce, polygamy, concubinage, polyandry and even promiscuity among various peoples. But these are all abnormalities. True happiness, true fulfillment, true accomplishment of God's purposes necessarily involve obedience to God's primal command. "Therefore shall a man leave his father and his mother, and shall *cleave* unto his wife: and they shall be *one flesh*."

We recognize, of course, that because of the entrance of sin into the world, it has not always been possible to adhere to the ideal. God Himself has seemed to sanction, or at least to allow, polygamy at times — witness the case of David and others in Old Testament days, whom God blessed and used in spite of their many wives. Similarly, the Mosaic law allowed divorce. In some cases God, even commanded divorce (Ezra 10:11).

But, as the Lord Jesus said: "From the beginning it was not so" (Matthew 19:8). With the full light of the Gospel and the New Testament Scriptures, the believing Christian who seeks to do the Lord's will in all things will certainly desire to follow His will in this most basic and important of all earthly relationships.

The Meaning of Marriage
(Genesis 2:23–25)

The marriage relation is thus seen to be of profound importance in God's terrestrial economy. It is not to be secularized or abused. It is a "joining together" by God Himself (Matthew 19:6), and is the basic means by which man was intended to accomplish God's purposes in the earth as His vice-regent (Genesis 1:28).

When God brought Eve to Adam, the man exclaimed: "This is now bone of my bones, and flesh of my flesh: she shall be called Woman [Hebrew *isha*], because she was taken out of man [Hebrew *ish*]." This is the first time this particular word is used for "man." Earlier the Hebrew *adham* had been used exclusively.

Thus Adam is truly the head of the race; even Eve was taken out of him. "Adam was first formed, then Eve" (I Timothy 2:13). "For the man is not of the woman; but the woman of the man. Neither was the man created for the woman; but the woman for the man" (I Corinthians 11:8, 9).

We may note in passing here that the New Testament clearly accepts the account of Adam and Eve in Genesis as actual history, to be taken literally. Those modern theologians (and they are many, even nowadays in certain "evangelical" circles) who regard Adam and Eve as merely allegorical, are thus in rebellion against the inspired testimony of Paul and even of the Lord Jesus (Matthew 19:4, 5; Mark 10:6–8). This is no light matter.

God must have had some reason for forming woman in this way, since it certainly was not the most obvious way of doing it, at least from our natural viewpoint. From references and inferences in the New Testament, it seems that there are certain great spiritual truths which God was showing forth in a type or pattern here, as well as the more immediately meaningful truth that Adam and Eve were truly "one flesh" and should thus serve their Creator together in unity and singleness of the heart.

As the first bridegroom and bride, Adam and Eve have become a "type" of all subsequent bridegrooms and brides, and especially of the heavenly Bridegroom, Jesus Christ (John 3:29; Matthew 25: 1–10) and His bride, the church (Revelation 21:9; II Corinthians 11:2; Ephesians 5:22–33).

Thus, Christ offered up His body to God (Hebrews 10:10) and entered the deep sleep of death. His side was pierced, as was Adam's, and His lifeblood came forth, mingled with water (John 19:34), testifying of the Spirit who brings regeneration — new life out of death (I John 5:6; I Peter 3:18). By both the redeeming blood (Acts 20:28) and the cleansing, life-giving water (Ephesians 5:25, 26), Christ gave Himself as the sacrifice to form the church as His bride and, indeed, as His own spiritual Body — bone of His bones and flesh of His flesh (Ephesians 5:30). In symbol, it is significant that the "life of (Adam's) flesh (was) in the blood" (Leviticus 17:11) and the blood is about 90% water — indeed all human flesh is over 60% water.

When Adam awoke from his deep sleep, and when God had finished forming Eve, He "brought her unto the man" (Genesis 2:22), to be with him from that time forth. In like manner, God is now forming a bride for Christ (Acts 15:14), as it were "building up the body" (Ephesians 4:11–16). When this work is completed, God will bring His bride to the Lord Jesus and He will go out to meet her, and she will be evermore joined to the Lord (John 14:2, 3; I Thessalonians 4:16, 17; Revelation 19:7-9; 21:1-4).

All of these truths of course are also typified by every true home, built on the pattern established by God. This is the truth so beautifully portrayed in the classic passage, Ephesians 5:22—33, where wives are exhorted to "submit yourselves unto your own husbands, *as unto the Lord,*" and husbands to "love your wives, even as Christ also loved the church and *gave himself for it.*"

As a matter of fact, the family unit ordained by God when he created man and woman is also itself a beautiful type of the *heavenly* family. Paul says, concerning the "Father of our Lord Jesus Christ," that it is of Him that "every family in heaven and earth is named" (Ephesians 3:15). Thus, the family unit should, if truly functioning according to the purpose of God, represent also the heavenly family. God is "our Father, which art in heaven." The Son of God was loved by the Father "before the foundation of the world" (John 17:24). "But when the fullness of the time was come, God sent forth His Son, made of a woman ... that we might receive the adoption of sons. And because ye are sons, God sent forth the Spirit of his Son into your hearts, crying, Abba, Father" (Galatians 4:4-6).

The mystery is too great for us to understand or explain. But somehow we know in our hearts that this is so. In our human families, at least in those where God is honored and His Word is believed, "through faith we understand" that the love of husband and wife and parents and children somehow shows forth the eternal love of the Father, Son and Holy Spirit, and the redeeming love of Christ for the church.

Questions for Discussion

1. How can one harmonize the creation of Eve out of Adam's side with the theory of human evolution?

2. What does the Genesis account of the origin of marriage teach with regard to divorce? How did Jesus answer this question?

3. Are polygamous marriages, common-law marriages or homosexual marriages ever legitimate in God's sight?

4. Explain how Adam was able to name the animals in just part of one day's time. How many did he have to name?

5. Explain the seeming contradiction between Genesis 1 and 2 in relation to the order of creation of man and the animals.

6. Does man have a responsibility before God to care for the animals and the general environment? Explain.

7. Is it legitimate in God's sight to use animals for research?

Chapter 5

The Problem of Evil

Genesis 3:1–19

When God's six-day work of creation was complete, everything in the world was "very good" (Genesis 1:31). There was nothing out of order, no suffering, no pain, no sin, and no death. Universal peace and harmony prevailed in all God's creation.

But this is *not* the way the world is now! In the physical realm, everything tends to run down and wear out. In the sphere of organic life, each animal is engaged in a perpetual struggle against other animals and against disease, as well as the universal process of aging and death. Sociologically and culturally, one civilization after another seems to rise for a time, then decline and die. In the spiritual and moral realm everyone finds that it is easier to do wrong than right, and to drift downwards than to struggle upwards. Something is fundamentally and seriously *wrong* with the world.

The problem of the existence of evil in a world created by a holy God is one that has exercised the minds and hearts of philosophers and theologians through the ages. If God is all-powerful and all-righteous, why does He permit sin and suffering and death in His creation? How, indeed, could evil ever have appeared at all? These questions do not have easy answers. Atheism in fact, is largely founded on the pessimistic answer that an evil world proves either that God is not good or that God is not powerful. The philosophy of dualism pro poses an eternal principle of evil in the universe, as well as one of good. But such answers as these, of course are neither Scriptural nor satisfying to man's heart-needs. God *is* omnipotent and He *is* perfectly righteous. Only His own revelation, therefore, can enable us to understand the source and significance of evil in the world.

At the end of the six days of creation, and for an indeterminate time after that, there was apparently no evil in the entire universe. Even Satan himself was originally "perfect in his ways" (Ezekiel 28:15). When God "laid the foundations of the earth," then "… the morning stars sang together and all the sons of God shouted for joy" (Job 38:4,7). An "innumerable company of angels" (Hebrews 12:22) joined in with their Creator, the triune God, in acknowledging the perfections and glories of His creation.

The angels (meaning "messengers") were evidently created for a variety of ministries around God's throne, and had various ranks and authorities — "principalities and powers." Michael, for example, is called the "archangel" (Jude 9; Revelation 12:7) and also "one of the chief princes" (Daniel 10:13). Gabriel is said to "stand in the presence of God" (Luke 1:19). Evidently the greatest of all these created beings was one called Lucifer ("day-star").

The Fall (Genesis 3:1–13)

Lucifer is spoken of in Isaiah 14:12–15, a passage which refers initially to the wicked "king of Babylon" but which also exposes the evil one who indwelt and energized him. Similarly Ezekiel 18:11–19 is addressed superficially to the "king of Tyre" but penetrates to the one who also possessed and empowered him.

Somehow Lucifer began to doubt God's Word. "His heart was lifted up because of his beauty and he corrupted his wisdom by reason of his brightness." God had told him he was "created" but the only knowledge he had of this was God's Word, and this he now preferred not to believe. He said in his heart: "I will be like the Most High" (Isaiah 14:14). He seems to have deceived himself into believing that both he and God were of similar kind and origin and therefore, that there was really no one who could have "created" either of them. All had somehow developed or evolved out of prior materials and it was only an accident of priority of time that placed him, with all his wisdom and beauty, beneath God in the angelic hierarchy.

And so began Satan's age-long attempt to thwart and defeat God's purposes and ultimately to "exalt his own throne above the stars of God" (Isaiah 14:13). Many other angels, possibly a third of them, followed him in his rebellion (Revelation 12:4, 9).

Because "iniquity was found in him," Satan fell "as lightning from heaven" (Luke 10:18). God "cast him to the earth" (Ezekiel 28:17) and ultimately he will be "brought down to hell" (Isaiah 14:15; Matthew 25:41).

On the earth, he was now in man's dominion. He knew that God had a glorious purpose and destiny for man, created "in his own image," and in his hatred for God, he immediately undertook to destroy that "image" and defeat God's purpose for man. Perhaps he believed that, by capturing man's dominion and affection, along with the allegiance of his own angels, he might even yet be able to ascend back to Heaven and dethrone God.

Thus Lucifer, the "day-star," became Satan the "adversary" or "accuser," opposing and calumniating God and all His purposes. And now he became "that old serpent" (Revelation 12:9; 20:2); entering into the body of the "most subtil" or "clever" of the various "beasts of the field" in order to approach Eve with his evil solicitations.

There have been numerous speculations about this serpent. Some have suggested that the word originally meant "shining, upright creature," and that the primeval appearance of the serpent was attractive and semi-human, before God's curse fell on it. Others suggest that the animals, at least the higher animals, were originally able to carry on verbal conversations with man, on a "soulual" (not a "spiritual") level. The most that can be said about such theories is that no actual evidence exists one way or the other.

Of course, the most important thing is the fact of the temptation, and its nature. It is profoundly significant that it began by Satan implanting a doubt concerning God's Word and His sovereign goodness. "Indeed," he said, in effect, "Did God *really* tell you that you mustn't eat this delicious fruit of the trees here in your garden?"

This approach was a masterpiece of subtlety. In this way, Satan conveyed the idea that it was possible to doubt God's Word and to question God's will and His goodness. Such doubts really are raising the question whether God is *really* God! Satan was seeking to plant his own unbelief in the mind of Eve, and he succeeded only too well.

This was the first beginning of sin in the human family. It succeeded so well that Satan and his evil spirits continue to use this approach today. If he can just get a person to begin, even in the slightest degree, to doubt God's Word or His sovereign goodness, then it is easy to go on, step by step, until that person is either openly rebellious against God or else utterly unable to accomplish God's purpose in his life. How blasphemous for one who is a *creature* of God to question in any respect what his Creator has said or done!

This is eminently instructive for the believer today who would be forewarned against Satan's wiles. The best defense is a strong offense. The Christian's armor (Ephesians 6:13–17) is *above all* the "shield of faith, wherewith ye shall be able to quench all the fiery darts of the wicked (one)."

If Eve had only replied to Satan with what God had *really* said! She left out God's "freely" and "every" when she said "We may eat of the fruit of the trees of the garden," thus undervaluing God's goodness and generosity (compare Genesis 2:16), and she magnified God's restriction by adding the unwarranted clause: "... neither shall ye touch it." How important it is to take God's Word just as it is, neither taking from it nor adding to it (Revelation 22:18, 19)!

Thus she was softened for the final blow Satan convinced her that God was selfishly restraining her from equality with Himself, "knowing good and evil." She was overcome (see I John 2:15–17) with the "lust of the flesh" (the tree was good for food), the "lust of the eyes" (it was pleasant to look upon), and the "pride of life" (it would make her wish).

And Adam in his turn "hearkened unto the voice of his wife" (Genesis 3:17) instead of the Word of God, and also ate the forbidden fruit.

But then, as they waited, expecting the coming of the promised wisdom, there came over them instead the realization of that they had done and an awful sense of shame enveloped them. As they remembered that their divine purpose had been to "multiply and fill the earth," they realized that the very fountain head of future human life had now become corrupted by their disobedience and they became acutely aware of their nakedness. Hastily they fashioned crude girdles of fig leaves and covered themselves, but of course such crude aprons would hardly suffice to hide the guilt of their rebellion against God. Neither will the "filthy rags" of our own self-made "righteousness" serve to cover our sinful hearts today (Isaiah 64:6). We need rather the "garments of salvation," the "robe of righteousness" (Isaiah 61:10) with which only God can clothe us (Genesis 3:21).

No longer did Adam and Eve enjoy the fellowship with God for which they had been created. Rather they "hid themselves," and then even made excuses for avoiding God's presence. And so rapidly did sin pervade their lives that, when God began to question them, Adam blamed his wife, and Eve blamed the serpent, neither willing to acknowledge his own guilt. In fact, Adam, by implication, cast the blame on God, emphasized that it was all because of "the woman whom *thou gavest to be with me.*" Instead of praising God for His goodness, he blamed Him for his troubles! How foolish and wicked — and how much like ourselves!

The Curse (Genesis 3:14-19)

The record does not imply that there was any physical ingredient in the fruit of the tree of knowledge which led to physical deterioration and death, though this may be a possibility. The real poison, corrupting the soul and killing the spirit, was the consciousness of guilt and the fear of death. Adam and Eve fled from God's presence and hid among the trees, and even tried to hide themselves, as it were, by fashioning fig-leaf girdles. But God, in grace, searched them out and elicited confessions from them. Then, in both justice and mercy, He imposed a divine curse on man and all his dominion — a curse which was fully appropriate to man's fallen state, but which also was calculated to show man his desperate need of the Saviour whom God would yet provide.

God pronounced His anathemas on the serpent, on Eve, and on Adam, in the chronological order of their respective acts of transgression. The serpent as an animal was cursed above all others in the animal kingdom, not because of direct culpability on his part, but rather as a perpetual reminder to man of the instrument of his fall and of the final destruction of Satan himself. The curse on Satan (Genesis 3:15) will be discussed more fully in the next chapter.

Eve shared in the curse on Adam, since she was also "of the man," but in addition a special curse was placed on her in connection with the experience of conception and childbirth, the pain and sorrow of which would be "greatly multiplied." It had been appointed to her to be the "mother of all living"

(Genesis 3:20), but now all her children to all generations would suffer under the curse. Their very entrance into the world would he marked by unique suffering, serving as a perpetual reminder of the dread effects of sin.

The curse on Adam was different in that it was more directly a curse on his dominion. "Cursed is the ground (same word as "earth," and meaning the basic material of the physical creation) for thy sake" (Genesis 3:17).

The earth which had previously cooperated readily as the man "tilled" and "dressed" it (Genesis 2:5, 15), now became reluctant to yield his food. Instead it yielded thorns and noxious weeds, requiring toil and sweat and tears before man could "eat of it." And finally, in spite of all his struggle, death would finally triumph and man's body would return to the dust from which it was taken.

Thus, as Paul says in Romans 8:20–22, the "creation was made subject to vanity" (or "futility"), and is now "groaning and travailing together in pain." The earth is "waxing old, like a garment" and "shall perish" (Hebrews 1:10–12). Since all flesh is made of the earth's physical elements, it also is subject to the law of decay and death. "All flesh is as grass, and all the glory of man as the flower of grass. The grass withereth and the flower thereof falleth away" (I Peter 1:24). The whole creation has been delivered into the "bondage of corruption" (literally "decay"). It is universal experience that all things, living or non-living, eventually wear out, run down, grow old, decay, and pass into the dust.

This condition is so worldwide that it was formalized about a hundred years ago (by Carnot, Clausius, Kelvin and other scientists) into a fundamental scientific law, now called the second law of thermodynamics. It says that all systems, if left to themselves, tend to become degraded or disordered. It has also been called the law of morpholysis (from a Greek word meaning "loosing of structure"). Physical systems, whether watches or suns, eventually wear out. Biological organisms grow old and die. Hereditary changes in species are caused by gene mutations, which represent sudden disruptions in the highly ordered genetic structure of the germ cell, and which nearly always result in either death or deterioration of the species.

As noted before, this second law of thermodynamics is one of the two basic laws of modern science, more firmly established by empirical evidence and of more universal applicability than any other scientific principle. The term *entropy,* which is a mathematical term measuring the unavailable energy in a thermodynamic system, is used to denote the degree of randomness, or disorder, of any system, and the second law states that the entropy of a "closed system" always increases.

Science knows that this is true, but science, as such, has never been able to suggest *why* it is true. Somehow in a universe created by a rational, loving God, such a principle seems strangely out of place. Just what *is* it that has gone wrong with God's world?

The only true and reasonable answer to this problem is found here in the third chapter of Genesis. The Apostle Paul, referring to this chapter says: "Wherefore, as by one man sin entered into the world, and death by sin: and so death passed upon all men, for that all have sinned" (Romans 5:12). Later, he says: "For the creature (actually *creation*) was made subject to vanity (or "futility"), not willingly, but by reason of him who hath subjected the same in hope. Because the (creation) itself also shall be delivered from the bondage of corruption (or "decay") into the glorious liberty of the children of God. For we know that the whole creation groaneth and travaileth in pain together until now" (Romans 8:2–22).

Thus the Christian doctrines of the Fall of man and God's Curse on His creation are fundamental not only to an understanding of history but also to true Biblical theology. Liberal theologians may ridicule the supposedly naive story of the serpent and the forbidden fruit, and may completely reject the historicity of Adam and Eve if they wish, but they should clearly recognize that in so doing they are also rejecting the authority of the New Testament and the Apostles. Not only does the New Testament explicitly accept the events of Genesis 3 as historically true (note especially Romans 5:12–19; II Corinthians 11:3; I Timothy 2:13, 14; I Corinthians 5:21, 22), but the entire structure of Christian theology is built on this foundation. The very need for a Saviour presupposes that man has inherited a corrupt and sinful nature. If man is by nature always evolving and improving, then he is capable of "saving" himself. The atoning death of the Son of God, offering Himself as a redeeming sacrifice for man's sin, becomes meaningless if man is not even lost. It is thus of profound and eternal importance that the Christian understand and *believe* this tragic record of man's Fall and the coming of sin and death into the world.

God always fulfills both His promises and His warnings. He had told Adam that in the day he ate of the fruit of the one forbidden tree, "... dying, thou shalt die." He would begin to die immediately and finally die completely. Since Adam was appointed to exercise dominion over the earth, his dominion also would begin to "die." God placed a curse on the whole creation He had created.

The curse was three-fold, just as creation had been three-fold. As we have noted previously, there were three great creative acts. First, the physical materials of the universe — the heavens and the earth — were created (Genesis 1:1). Second the "living souls" — animals which possess conscious existence as distinct from plants which have only unconscious existence — were created. Third, man possessing soul (self-consciousness) and spirit (capacity for fellowship with God) was created in the image of God (Genesis 1:27). The other great events of the creation week all consisted of processes of forming, ordering and organizing the *created* entities into various "kinds" of physical and biological "bodies" (I Corinthians 15:38–41).

But now God cursed the physical earth, the "ground" (Genesis 3:18), from whose elements the various bodies had been formed. Similarly, the animals were cursed, and especially the serpent, who was "cursed" *above* all cattle and *above* every beast of the field," (Genesis 3:14). as a perpetual reminder to man of the promised eventual destruction of the evil one who had used his body.

And the curse fell hardest of all on man. This curse was fourfold as follows: (1) *Sorrow,* resulting from continual disappointment and futility; (2) *pain and suffering,* signified by the "thorns" which intermittently hinder man in his efforts to provide a living for his family; (3) *sweat,* or tears the "strong crying" of intense struggle against a hostile environment; and finally (4) physical *death,* which would eventually triumph over all man's efforts, with the structure of his body returning to the simple elements of the earth.

But Christ, as Son of Man and second Adam, has been made the curse for us. He was the "man of *sorrows*" (Isaiah 53:3), acquainted more with grief than any other man; He was "wounded, bruised, and chastised" for us (Isaiah 53:5) and indeed wore the very *thorns* of the curse as His crown; in the agony of His labor, He *sweat* as it were drops of blood, and "offered up prayers and supplications with strong cryings and tears" (Hebrews 5:7). And finally, God brought Him "into the *dust of death*" (Psalm 22:15).

"Delivered unto glorious liberty!" Because Christ suffered for us, once again the dwelling of God shall someday be with men and "there shall be to more *death,* neither *sorrow,* nor *crying,* neither shall there be any more *pain*: for the former things are passed away" (Revelation 21:4). "And there shall be no more curse: but the throne of God and of the Lamb shall be in it: and His servants shall serve Him" (Revelation 22:3).

In addition to the curse on mankind in general, however, women were to be placed under a particular burden, because of Eve's sin. Her sorrow "especially in thy conception" would be "greatly multiplied" (Genesis 3:16). The function of reproduction and motherhood, originally given as the joyful fruition of God's purpose in her creation, but now marred so severely by her "lust" for withheld knowledge, which conceived and brought forth sin and death (James 1:15), would henceforth be marked by unique suffering in its accomplishment. Furthermore, she who had acted independently of her husband in her fateful decision to taste the desired fruit, must henceforth exercise her desire only to her husband and he would bear rule over her.

This, then, is the true origin of the strange law of disorder and decay, the second law of thermodynamics. Instead of all things being "made" — that is, organized into highly complex systems and structures — as they were in creation week, they are now being "unmade," becoming disorganized and simple. Instead of life and growth, there comes decay and death; instead of evolution, there is degeneration. Herein is the secret of all that's wrong with the world. Man is a sinner, and God's curse is upon the earth.

This law of increasing entropy, one of the two best-proved laws of science, precisely contradicts the idea of evolution. Evolution is believed to be a universal process in which things increase in order, whereas the second law of thermodynamics is a universal law of decreasing order. Each is the opposite of the other, so how can they both be true? This problem has been almost completely ignored by evolutionists, and has certainly never been resolved. Christians can be sure that "vertical" evolution is completely impossible, not only because the Bible says so, but also because the laws of science preclude it. Even though the Curse does speak of God's judgment on the earth, it also points to the fact of creation and a Creator, so that man is continually confronted with the fact that he is responsible to God. Furthermore, the principle of decay and death continually bears witness to him that he is insufficient in himself and needs a Saviour.

In our finite minds, we may not understand all about why God has allowed sin and suffering and death to enter His creation. But we can simply rest in faith in His divine wisdom and power. Somehow, He is bringing even greater glory to His Name, and greater blessing to His children, through His work of redemption and salvation than through His work of creation.

Questions for discussion

1. What is the relation of the scientitic concept of entropy to the theological implication of the curse?

2. How did the second law of thermodynamics function in nature before the fall and curse?

3. What are the implications of the curse in relation to evolution?

4. What is the basic cause and nature of sin?

5. Is the existence of evil and suffering in the world compatible with the gospel of Christ? If so, how?

6. How can a God of love and power allow injustice and suffering to continue existing in the world?

7. What was the basic temptation Satan used (and still uses) to cause men to sin?

Chapter 6

The Promised Redeemer

Genesis 3:15–4:15

From the very day when man first sinned and first realized that he had come under God's curse, God has also been promising a Saviour. Both in symbolic parallels (or "types") and in direct prophecies, God has over and over again indicated that some day One would come who would vanquish Satan, redeem man, reconcile him to God, remove the curse from the world and bring to glorious fruition all of God's purposes in creation. Even in the very act of pronouncing the curse, God simultaneously promised the coming Deliverer. This wonderful promise is found in Genesis 3:15 and is known as the Protevangel (meaning "first gospel"). In this one verse is a capsule summary of all human history. The warfare between the "seed of the serpent" and the "seed of the woman" is truly the conflict of the ages.

As noted in the previous chapter, God's curse was pronounced on the serpent, the woman, and the man in that order. But between the curse on the serpent and on the woman is interjected a prophecy of continuing enmity between the serpent and the woman and their respective seeds. "I will put enmity between thee and the woman, and between thy seed and her seed; it (or "he") shall bruise (or "crush") thy head and thou shalt bruise his heel."

The Promise of Salvation (Genesis 3:15–24)

The earth had been originally placed under man's dominion. By persuading them to follow his word instead of God's Word, Satan probably believed that he had now won the allegiance of the first man and woman and therefore also of all their descendants. They would be allies of himself and his host of evil angels in their efforts to dethrone and vanquish God. Satan was now the "god of this world" (II Corinthians 4:4), and the woman especially, who was to bear the earth's future children, would readily follow him. She had already demonstrated her control over the man, who had eaten of the fruit when she told him to, even though he himself was not deceived. With the wonderful potentialities of human reproduction under his control, Satan could, as it were, in time "create" an innumerable host of obedient servants to do his bidding.

But if such thoughts as these were in Satan's mind, he was not only the "deceiver of the whole world" (Revelation 12:9), but he himself was deceived most of all. The woman, in the first place would *not* become his willing ally. "I will put *enmity* between thee and the woman," God said. Neither would she rule over her husband. "Her desire shall be to her husband, and he shall rule over her." Conception and childbirth would not be easy and rapid. "I will greatly multiply the woman's sorrow, especially in conception; in sorrow will she bring forth children."

Not only would victory not be as easy as he had thought, but ultimately he would be completely defeated and destroyed. "There will come One who will not be of the man's seed, and who therefore will not be under your dominion. He will be uniquely the Seed of the woman, virgin-born. Though you will succeed in grievously injuring Him, He will completely crush you and all your evil ambitions!"

This is obviously more than a reference to the *physical* enmity between men and snakes, although this may be included. The serpent as an animal was only the vehicle that Satan used. The real burden of the prophecy, as a part of God's curse, must therefore have been directed against Satan himself. The prophecy thus looks forward to a time when Satan shall be completely crushed beneath the feet of the woman's triumphant seed.

But first there is seen a time of conflict and even apparent victory on the part of the serpent, who is able to "bruise the heel" of the woman's seed. This predicted conflict is reflected in the legends and mythologies of the ancients, filled as they are with tales of heroes engaged in life-and-death struggles with serpents and dragons and other monsters. The star-figures by which early peoples identified the heavenly constellations repeat the same story, especially in the so-called "signs of the Zodiac" and their accompanying "decans." There is the picture, for example, of Hercules battling with the serpent. The constellation Virgo, with the spike of wheat in her hands, may refer to the promised "seed of the woman." The king of animals, Leo, is shown clawing the head of a great, fleeing serpent. The Scorpion is illustrated as stinging the heel of the great hero Ophiuchus.

These and many similar representations of the ancient myths may well be somewhat distorted remembrances of this great primeval prophecy. Mankind, from the earliest ages, has recorded its hope that some day a Saviour would come who would destroy the devil and reconcile man to God.

But who, or what, is meant by the "seed of the serpent" and the "seed of the woman"? The term "seed" has a biological connotation, of course, but is used here in a somewhat paradoxical manner. Neither Satan, who is a spirit nor the woman would be able to produce actual biological "seed" — only the man was created physically to do this. This seed is therefore primarily a spiritual progeny or offspring.

Specifically, it appears that Satan's seed consists of those who knowingly and willfully set themselves at enmity with the seed of the woman. They partake in a very specific sense of the character of the Adversary, and seek to oppose and defeat God's purposes in creation and redemption.

The "seed of the woman," on the other hand, would refer to those in the human family who are brought into right relationship with God through faith, children of the Father. Thus two spiritual progenies are before us in the terms "seed of the serpent," and "seed of the woman."

However, this generalized application of the conflict of the two spiritual seeds has also a much more specific application as well. It is clear that there is a definite personal conflict predicted between Satan himself and one who would become the Seed of the women in an actual physical sense, with the latter ultimately triumphant.

One could be a *physical* seed of woman only if there were no male seed involved in conception. This would require a miraculous conception and birth in a virgin's womb. Thus, in this great promise, God also prophesied that the coming Deliverer would be supernaturally conceived and born of a virgin. Such a promised Seed would not partake of the inherited sin-nature of Adam's children, but would nevertheless be true man born of woman. He would not be born under Satan's dominion as would other men, and thus would be able to engage that old serpent in mortal conflict. Finally, though bruised in the conflict, He would emerge the Victor, destroying Satan and setting the captives free!

This promise is of course fulfilled in Jesus Christ! He appeared to be mortally bruised when He died on the cross, but He rose again and soon will return to cast the devil into the lake of fire (Revelation 20:10). And in His very dying, "bruised for our iniquities" (Isaiah 53:5), He satisfied the just requirements of God's holiness. He died for the sin of Adam, and therefore also for the sin of all who were "in Adam." "For as in Adam all die, even so in Christ shall all be made alive" (I Corinthians 15:22).

As it relates to Christ in particular, there is probably an implied reference to this prophecy in Isaiah 7:14, which should read: "Therefore the Lord Himself shall give you a sign: behold *the* virgin shall conceive and bear a son, and shall call his name Immanuel." The definite article before "virgin," which is present in the Hebrew text, indicates one that was previously promised. Similarly in Jeremiah 31:22. "For the Lord hath created a new thing in the earth, a women shall compass a man." An ordinary conception would not be a *new* thing.

The great sign which John saw in Heaven (Revelation 12:1–17) points to the final fulfillment of the prophecy. The woman seems here to represent the chosen nation Israel, in general, and Mary the mother of Jesus in a specific sense, although she may also be understood to symbolize all the true people of God. The man-child is Christ and the Dragon is that old Serpent waiting to destroy Him. But He is caught up into the heavens and the Serpent, defeated in his attempt to destroy the true Seed, angrily continues to "make war with the remnant of her seed, which keep the commandments of God and have the testimony of Jesus Christ." Finally, the Dragon is to be bound in the abyss for a thousand years, and eventually cast into the lake of fire (Revelation 20:2, 10).

When God proclaimed this "first Gospel" to Adam and Eve, promising salvation in spite of their sin and the resultant curse, there is evidence that, this time, they *believed* God's Word. "Adam called his wife's name Eve; because she was the mother of all living," thus indicating his faith that God would indeed send the promised seed of the woman.

In response to their faith, God graciously provided a covering for their nakedness. Their self-made fig-leaf aprons were entirely inadequate, so God made "coats of skins, and clothed them" (Genesis 3:21). Perhaps they silently and sorrowfully watched as God selected two of their animal friends, probably two sheep, and slew them there shedding the innocent blood before their eyes. They learned, in type, that an "atonement" (or "covering") could only be provided by the shedding of blood upon the altar (note Leviticus 17:11). We do not know, of course, but it may be that the experience also taught them that the woman's promised Seed must eventually shed His blood in the awful conflict that was coming, before the *full* atonement could be provided. In any case, they were soon to experience the reality of this conflict in the tragic history of their first two sons.

The garden of Eden continued to exist for an unknown length of time after the expulsion of Adam and Eve. The tree of life still grew there, and man was driven from the garden in order to prevent him from eating of its fruit any longer. The implication is that this fruit contained ingredients with the power of inhibiting cellular decay and the other degenerative bodily processes which culminate in physical death. It is interesting to note that God will again plant the tree of life in the new earth which He will create (Revelation 2:7; 22:2).

To "keep" (or "guard") the way of the tree of life, God placed at the east of the garden two cherubim, with a revolving, flaming sword. These creatures, among the highest in the angelic hierarchy, are described more fully in Ezekiel 1:4–28, Ezekiel 10:1–22 and Revelation 4:6–8. Satan himself had once been the "anointed cherub" (Ezekiel 28:14) upon God's holy mountain.

The cherubim are always associated closely with the throne of God, and it is thus intimated that God's presence was particularly manifest there at the tree of life. Later, His presence was especially revealed over the mercy-seat in the Holy of holies in the tabernacle (Exodus 25:17–22; Hebrews 9:3–5), and it is significant that this "mercy-seat" was overshadowed and guarded, as it were, by the figures of two golden cherubim. It was here that, once each year, the high priest entered with the sacrificial blood of atonement to sprinkle over the mercy-seat (see Leviticus 16; Hebrews 9:7–9; 24–28).

By analogy, it may have been that it was here, between the cherubim guarding the way to the tree of life, that God continued at intervals to meet with Adam and those of his descendants who desired to know Him.

The Conflict of the Ages (Genesis 4:1–15)

The story of Cain and Abel, while in every way to be understood as actual history, is also a parable of the age-long conflict of the two seeds. Cain typifies the "seed of the serpent," while Abel is a type of Christ, the "seed of the woman." In a secondary sense, he represents also those who, by faith, are "in Christ," and who therefore also are in a spiritual sense "seed of the woman."

When Cain was born, Eve exclaimed "I have gotten a man from the Lord!" Quite possibly she hoped that this might be the promised Deliverer, even though he was not in a specific sense a "seed of the woman." But as a matter of fact, "he was of that wicked one" (1 John 3:12), and thus was the first in the line of the serpent's seed.

His younger brother, Abel, was truly in the line of faith, however. He is the very first mentioned in the long line of men of faith as recorded in Hebrews 11 (verse 4). He is called "righteous" and "a prophet" (Matthew 23:35; Luke 11:50, 51), by Christ Himself.

By clear implication, therefore, Abel believed and obeyed God's Word, and righteousness was thus imputed to him. As a prophet, he must also have received God's Word by divine revelation and preached it by divine enablement. But Cain refused it and disobeyed.

As the boys grew, Cain became a farmer and Abel a shepherd. Both were honorable occupations, Cain's fruits providing food and Abel's sheep providing clothing for the family. In addition, it is evident that the sheep were to be used for sacrifice. The lesson which God had taught Adam and Eve was not to be forgotten. Atonement required the shedding of blood.

If our inferences are correct, God had made gracious provision to continue to commune with man, even though now "at a distance," on the basis of His promise of a coming Redeemer, whose shed blood would be the price of redemption. He had also showed man that an "atonement" required the shedding of innocent blood to provide a "covering" for the guilty. Probably at an appointed time and place, men were able to meet God, first being careful to approach Him by means of a proper offering, especially marked by the substitutionary shedding of blood. Those who "worshiped" (that is, "bowed down" to God's will in this way thus acknowledged their own guilt and helplessness and their trust in God alone for complete salvation and provision. There was nothing in this process appealing to the physical, or aesthetic, or mental appetites of man (as contrasted with Satan's appeal to Eve — Genesis 3:6), and thus it required the complete subjugation of human pride to the will of God.

One's attitude of heart towards this matter of approaching and knowing God actually determines his destiny in eternity. If he willingly accepts God's Word, approaching Him on the basis solely of faith in God's provision, through the shed blood of the Redeemer, God's Lamb, then he is spiritually of the heaven-born "seed of the woman" and he is restored to God's presence and fellowship. But if he continues to distort and reject God's Word, relying on his own personal merits to earn salvation, he is then in effect interposing his own will in place of God's — he is "as gods, knowing good and evil," — and thus becomes of the serpent's seed.

The enmity of the old Serpent poisoned Cain's soul when God would not receive his gift, and it would not rest until Abel's blood was shed.

"The voice of thy brother's blood crieth unto me from the ground" (Genesis 3:10). For the first time, "blood" is actually mentioned in the Bible, although its significance had been intimated several times previously. Abel, the type of the seed of the woman, was righteous before God and yet died violently at the hand of the first of the serpent's seed. Abel, as a prophet of God, had undoubtedly been urging his brother to approach God in His ordained way. Cain violently stilled his voice but now must listen to "the voice of thy brother's *blood.*"

This same conflict reached a tragic crescendo when those religious leaders whom Christ said were "of your father the devil" (John 8:44, Matthew 23:15) cried out for His crucifixion, hissing: "His blood be on us and on our children" (Matthew 27:25).

But the blood of Christ "speaketh better thing than that of Abel" (Hebrews 12:24). The blood of animals could never really take away sin, though it might enable their skins to be used for a temporary covering. But "the blood of Jesus Christ, God's Son, cleanseth us from all sin" (I John 1:7).

This conflict between the two spiritual seeds continues today and is rapidly heading toward its final climax. The present time *seems* to be one of imminent victory for Satan.

Though Satan's final defeat awaits the glorious coming of Christ, we have His promise even now of spiritual victory in our current conflicts with him. "And the God of peace shall bruise Satan under your feet shortly. The grace of our Lord Jesus Christ be with you. Amen" (Romans 16:20).

God's punishment of Cain is thus also a type of the ultimate crushing of the head of the serpent, when he will be separated forever from God in the lake of fire. Cain was forever "driven out from the presence of the Lord" (verses 14, 16); likewise shall all those who obey not the Gospel of Christ "be punished with everlasting destruction from the presence of the Lord, and from the glory of his power" (II Thessalonians 1:9).

Furthermore, Cain could no longer produce the fruits by which he had sought to approach God. The earth would no longer yield its increase for him, and he must become a "wanderer" in the earth. In like manner, those who attempt to earn salvation by their good works find ultimately that, of themselves, they can produce "thorns and thistles" — the true "good works" are those which God works in us through faith (note Ephesians 2:8–10). Though God allowed Cain to live for a time in the earth, just as today He lets the "tares and the wheat," the good seed and the bad seed grow together until the time of harvest (Matthew 13:24–30; 36–43), yet his ultimate fate, as one who had "known the way of righteousness," but had "turned from the holy commandment delivered unto him" (II Peter 2:21), is condemnation.

Questions for Discussion

1. Is the first gospel (or protevangel, as it is called) different from the gospel of Christ? If so, how? If not how are they similar?

2. Why do people wear clothing, while animals do not?

3 When was the first blood shed in the world, and what was its spiritual significance?

4. Discuss the concept of the "two seeds," as it unfolded through history.

5. How is Abel a type of Christ? Discuss the references in the New Testament to Cain and Abel.

6. Who were the cherubim at the entrance to the Garden of Eden, and what is their function in the divine economy?

7. What is the significance of the phrase "seed of the woman" in relation to the promised coming of Christ?

Chapter 7

The Lost World

Genesis 4:16–5:32

Almost forgotten by the world of modern scholarship, a mighty civilization once thrived over much of the earth. There is a kernel of truth in the many traditions of a former world, or of a legendary Golden Age, or of a sunken Atlantis, which the ethnologist encounters so frequently in his researches. This was the world before the Flood, the world of Adam and Enoch, of Cain and Lamech, Methuselah and Noah. These were real people and they built a great civilization, but their world was completely destroyed (note II Peter 3:5) by the Flood. Therefore, the only reliable records which we have of it are those preserved in the Bible, supported by the more or less distorted information also available in ancient traditions. But the Biblical record of this lost civilization is both scientifically, and spiritually significant, as we shall see in this chapter.

Were it not for the "book of the generations" of Adam (Genesis 5:1) and of Noah (Genesis 6:9), there would be no reliable history available of the antediluvian period. There are, of course, many traditions of a vanished civilization, but these have all become grossly distorted in transmission, and only become meaningful in light of the outline preserved for us in the Bible. As noted before, it appears reasonable that the records of Adam, Noah, and others, were carefully handed down from each patriarch to his successor until they finally came into the possession of Moses, who organized them into our present book of Genesis. Although the Biblical record of this era is quite brief, enough information is given to provide a fairly clear picture of its main characteristics.

The Antediluvian Civilization
(Genesis 4:16–24)

During the period from the Fall to the Flood, there seems to have been no organized system of laws or government for controlling human conduct. However, Adam undoubtedly instructed his sons and daughters (Genesis 5:4) concerning the curse, as well as God's promise of a coming Redeemer and His provision for approaching Him through blood sacrifice.

There were some, especially those in the line of the patriarchs listed in Genesis 5, who heeded Adam's counsel and thus believed and obeyed God's Word. But undoubtedly most were content to go "in the way of Cain," and it was not long before the "wickedness of man was great in the earth." Thus it has been demonstrated long ago that man cannot be simply left to live according to his own devices; laws and governments are absolutely necessary.

The antediluvian world was substantially different from that in which we now live. As intimated in Genesis 1:6, a considerable portion of the earth's waters then were stored "above the firmament" in the form of a vast blanket of invisible water vapor. This canopy would have produced a much more efficient "greenhouse effect" than the small vapor content of the present atmosphere is able to do. Even the latter, less than two inches in equivalent depth of rainfall, makes life possible on the earth by its relative equalizing of day and night temperatures. With the antediluvian vapor canopy, the earth must have enjoyed a uniform, mildly warm climate all year long and over its whole surface. The nearly constant temperatures would, in turn, have precluded the development of strong winds and storms. Rainfall as we know it was impossible and the necessary circulation of moisture for plant growth was accomplished by the spring-fed rivers and daily low-lying mists mentioned in Genesis 2:6, 10. These conditions undoubtedly contributed to the development of luxuriant growths of trees and other plants throughout the earth.

It is probable that the topography was fairly gentle. Most of the earth's present mountain ranges give evidence of extreme youthfulness and probably were uplifted after the Flood. With much of the earth's water above the atmosphere, the oceans were much smaller, probably occupying only about half the earth's surface. But the waters were warm and thus supported literally "swarms" of marine creatures (note Genesis 1:20, 21).

The vapor canopy probably also had the important effect of contributing to health and longevity by filtering out the deadly radiations bombarding the earth's surface from outer space. It is known that these rays are harmful and are a chief cause of mutations and other deteriorative activity in living flesh.

Whatever the physical explanation, the Scriptures indicate that antediluvian men lived to very great ages, and that most families were quite large. These two factors assured that God's primeval command to man to "be fruitful and multiply and fill the earth" (Genesis 1:28) would be rapidly carried out. At least one of Adam's sons had to marry one of his daughters (note Genesis 5:4) in order for the commanded racial proliferation to get started. The first families were thus necessarily formed from close relatives. At present, inbreeding is dangerous, because of the possible presence of harmful mutant genes in both parents, but this would have been no problem before any mutant genes had been established.

Thus the ancient quibble about "Cain's wife" is quite trivial. She as either his sister or a descendant of a sister and brother. The Bible does not say how old Cain was, or what the earth's population had become, at the time of his crime and punishment.

Cain "went out from the presence of the Lord," away from Eden, and settled in a region called Nod (meaning "wandering," probably referring to his punishment and manner of life). There he built the earth's first "city," which he named for his son, Enoch.

With the departure of Cain and his wife, it appears that, at least for a time, the Cainites and the Sethites developed more or less independently of each other. The descendants of Seth, Adam's third son, "appointed in place of Abel," continued to "call upon the name of the Lord," and probably attempted to maintain close obedience to the divine instructions given to Adam.

The Cainitic nation, on the other hand, seemed to retain very little concern for God and His will. It became enamored of comfort and pleasure and developed a culture evidently much like that of the world today, in kind if not in degree.

The longevity of the antediluvians was a major factor contributing to population expansion. No one even today really understands the aging process, except that it is associated with general bodily deterioration and decay. There is no inherent scientific reason why a human lifespan should normally be about seventy years instead of a thousand years. Suggested partial explanations for antediluvian longevity might include the following: (1) pristine purity of the racial genotype and its bloodstream, with few accumulated mutant genes; (2) harmonious nature of the primeval biosphere, only gradually corrupted, as a result of the outworking of the curse, into an environment containing disease-producing bacteria and other organisms harmful to man; (3) the congenial atmospheric environment, protected by the thermal vapor blanket (implied in Genesis 1:6) from temperature extremes and from radiations producing harmful mutations and other degenerative biologic processes.

Genes are very small particles, probably of molecular size, which exist in the germ cell and which serve to transmit the characteristics of parents to children. Occasionally, due to penetration of the germ cell by powerful radiations or chemicals, a gene may undergo a sudden change, or "mutation."

This will normally produce a disarrangement of the genetic system and thus will in some way damage the physiological structure of the child (or animal or plant) which contains it. Such genetic mutations are hereditary and thus the gradual accumulation of mutant genes in the race would eventually result in a deterioration of the racial stock as a whole.

Although we have no exact figures, it is possible to make a more or less reasonable guess as to how the population may have developed. Assuming that each family had only six children, and assuming that each generation (the time required for one cycle of birth, growth, marriage and childbearing) took 100 years, and also that the average lifespan was five generations, then the population at the end of Adam's 930 years of life would have been approximately 80,000. At the time of the Flood (1656 years after Adam's creation), the population would have been about 235,000,000 people. If a generation were 90 years instead of 100 years, the two numbers would be about 250,000 and 1,750,000,000, respectively. If each family had eight children per 100-year generation instead of six they would become one million and 25 billion, respectively!

Some have suggested that the "years" of the ages of the patriarchs may actually have been months. That this is impossible is obvious when the same suggestion is applied to their ages at the birth of their sons. Enoch, for example, would have been only five years old when Methuselah was born!

Not only did the population increase, but the technological and cultural level, at least of the Cainitic nation, seems to have been high. Metal tools of all kinds were available to produce creature comforts, and musical instruments were available to stimulate the emotional and aesthetic senses. Although these and other facets of civilization can be used for good purposes, they can easily become an end in themselves and can even be used as a means of rebelling against God. The latter seems to have been their effect, and perhaps even their purpose, among the descendants of Cain.

His descendants developed what may rightly be considered the worlds first civilization. As such, it is the prototype of all subsequent civilizations and cultures. Not only did Cainitic civilization introduce city life, with its implied community of inter-related activities and interests, but it also introduced nomadic life and the domestication and herding of cattle (Genesis 4:20). Technology seems to have begun with Tubal-cain, who was a forger who devised all kinds of things of bronze and iron (4:22) The musical arts began with Jubal, who invented the harp and organ (stringed instruments and wind instruments). Lamech may have been the first poet (4:23, 24).

Civilization's attempt to thwart the effects of God's curse is illustrated by the Cainitic economy as follows: (1) Urban life was preferred by many, instead of "tilling the ground"; (2) Nomadic life was preferred by others, instead of the settled dwelling-place required for agriculture; (3) Cattle raising was inaugurated, probably because men had become meat-eaters instead of being content with food grown from the earth; (4) Metal working and tools were developed to ease the "toil" of the curse; (5) Musical instruments were developed to mitigate the "sorrow"; (6) Poetic boasting, as noted in Lamech's song and as often characteristic of human poetry and writing, asserted man's self-sufficiency and independence of God; (7) Polygamy was introduced, instead of adhering to the monogamous form of marriage.

Lamech, in particular, representing the seventh generation of mankind on the Cainitic side (just as Enoch did on the Sethitic side), tragically reflects the spirit of his age. His character is revealed by the preserved fragment of a song he had composed and sung to his two wives, Adah and Zillah, boasting of his prowess in combat and his determination to visit mortal retribution on anyone presuming to oppose him. His blasphemous outburst against God is especially noteworthy. In punishing his ancestor Cain, God had nevertheless issued warning against killing Cain, stating that seven-fold punishment would overtake anyone doing so. But now Lamech says in effect: "Well, if *God* promises a seven-fold vengeance on anyone *killing* Cain, I myself guarantee a *seventy-seven-fold* retribution on anyone who even *hurts me!*"

One should contrast this attitude with that enjoined on us by Christ, who told Peter that he should forgive his brother not just seven times, or even seventy-seven times, but seventy times seven! (Matthew 18:21).

The Cainites evidently continued at least to believe in God, as indicated by the fact that two of the names of Cain's descendants end in the suffix *el*, which is the first syllable of *Elohim*, "God." However, it was only the Sethites who "called upon the name of the *Lord,*" which is the Hebrew *Jehovah*, the covenant and redemptive name of God.

Occasionally critics have noted certain similarities in the names of the respective descendants of Cain and Seth, and have said that the two lists are therefore corrupted remnants of one original list. Such a suggestion is, of course, entirely unacceptable. The few similarities that exist can perhaps be attributed to the occasional contacts that the two branches of the family must have maintained with each other. It is remarkable what a contrast in characters is evidenced by the Lamech in Cain's line with the Lamech in Seth's line!

It is probable that the name of the Roman god "Vulcan" was originally a corruption of the last part of the name "Tubal-cain," who evidently invented the smelting and working of metals, and probably also metallic weapons and implements of various kinds.

But with all the comforts of civilization and the cultural influences of the fine arts, the Cainites were nevertheless rebellious against God, and their civilization soon so corrupted the world that it had to be completely purged. As far as the record goes, none of the Cainites ever again sought "the presence of the Lord."

Instead of tilling the ground for food, in an agricultural economy, they chose to establish both urban and nomadic cultures. By the time of Lamech, if not earlier, God's establishment of monogamous marriage was no longer respected, and neither was the sacredness of human life.

The Patriarchal Testimony
(Genesis 4:25–5:32)

Although the Cainites revealed the flowering of the serpent's seed in the life of mankind, God was still maintaining the integrity of the line of the promised Seed of the woman. First, He appointed to Eve "another seed instead of Abel, whom Cain slew" (4:25). Then, in the days of Enos, the son of Seth, it is recorded that "men began to call upon the name of Jehovah" (4:26).

The exact meaning of this statement is somewhat uncertain. Possibly it signifies the beginning of public worship of the Lord in place of the previous practice of individually meeting with Him as Cain and Abel did. Perhaps it refers to the beginning of the practice of prayer, implying that God's immediate presence was no longer accessible.

In any case, it surely denotes an act of faith on the part of those who "called upon his name." In later times, and probably at this time, it was accompanied by the building of an altar and the offering of a sacrifice thereon (see Genesis 12:8; 13:4; 26:25; I Kings 18:23, 24). The name of Jehovah, representing all that He is and does, promising and providing salvation to all who trust His word, was regarded as unutterably sacred (Exodus 20:7; Leviticus 24:16).

Before Calvary, when God Himself provided one great sacrifice for sins forever, it was needful for men, as they called upon His name, again and again to offer their sacrifices, shedding the blood upon the altar as atonement for their souls (Leviticus 17:11). But *since* Calvary, men need now only to call in faith on the name of Jesus Christ as Lord, for eternal salvation. For "whosoever shall call on the name of the Lord shall be saved" (Joel 2:32; Acts 2:21; Romans 10:13). Jesus is not only the Christ (the "Anointed") and the promised Seed of the woman, but He is Himself the Lord, Jehovah, the eternal "I AM." He is the *Lord Jesus Christ!* "God hath given him *the* name which is above every name ... that every tongue should confess that Jesus Christ is Lord" (Philippians 2:9–11). There is a marked change in emphasis in the record of the descendants of Adam through Seth. No more do we read of human accomplishments or of violence and boasting. Rather, we read of men "calling upon the name of the Lord" (4:26), of Enoch "walking with the Lord" (5:24) and of Lamech prophesying of God's "comfort" despite the curse (5:29).

Nevertheless, the Sethites were members of a fallen race no less than the Cainites. In the first verse of Genesis 5 the writer recalls again that God created man "in the likeness of God." But then, in verse 3, he says Adam "begat a son in *his* own likeness, after *his* image; and called his name Seth." Between Adam and Seth intervened the Fall. Though Adam was *created* in God's image, Seth was *begotten* in Adam's image, and he therefore partook of the fallen nature of his father (note Romans 5: 12–14).

The first verse of Genesis 5 marks one of the major divisions of Genesis. It is significant that it says: "This is the *book* of the generations of Adam." The record thus was *written,* not just transmitted orally. Quite possibly, Adam himself wrote the section (chapters 2, 3, 4) which concludes with this statement, and Noah (note Genesis 6:9) recorded the genealogies of chapter 5.

It is interesting to note that the record of Cain's descendants stops with the deeds of Lamech, who was in the seventh generation from Adam. From the chronologies of Genesis 5, it is evident that Adam died about this time, during the lifetime of Enoch, who was also in the seventh generation from Adam.

The possession of a *written* language among the antediluvian is not only implied by the use of "book" in the above passage, but is in fact practically demanded by the high civilization of the Cainites. The development of cities, metallurgy, music, poetry, and other accoutrements of an advanced culture surely presupposes the ability to communicate by written symbols.

It is also interesting to note that while Genesis 5:1 contains the first mention of "book" (or, one might say, "Bible") in the Old Testament, the first mention of "book" in the New Testament is in Matthew 1:1, "the *book* of the generations of Jesus Christ." Thus, the *first* book tells of the origins of the first Adam; the *second* book speaks of the origins of the last Adam, who is "the Lord from heaven" (I Corinthians 15:47)!

The list of names and ages of the antediluvian patriarchs, which may seem superficially dull and monotonous, becomes meaningful and exciting on closer inspection. It tells us, for example, that men once were able to live almost a thousand years. The record also indicates that men were able to have children for hundreds of years (Enoch had a son at age 65 and Noah at age 500). But the record also indicates, repeatedly, that every man finally died. "It is appointed unto men once to die" (Hebrews 9:27).

Genesis 5:5 gives the obituary announcement of Adam's death fulfilling the physical aspect of the death sentence pronounced on him in Genesis 2:17 and assuring all that "the wages of sin is death" (Romans 6:23).

In spite of the curse, however, God was careful to preserve the line of the promised Seed. In all, there were ten antediluvian patriarchs in the lineage, as follows: Adam, Seth, Enos, Cainan, Mahalaleel, Jared, Enoch, Methuselah (the longest living person in antiquity), Lamech, and Noah. There is no reason to think that these men were all the *firstborn* sons of their fathers We know, for example, that Seth was Adam's *third* son, and we know that each of the patriarchs "begat sons and daughters." The names of those in the line of the promised Seed are the ones preserved, however.

A comparison of the dates of birth and death of the patriarchs, as given in Genesis 5 is instructive. The parentheses at (1) and (987) note that Adam was not actually born and Enoch did not die, for "God took him," in the years given.

	Year of Birth	Year of Death
Adam	(1)	930
Seth	130	1042
Enos	235	1140
Cainan	325	1235
Mahalaleel	395	1290
Jared	460	1422
Enoch	622	(987)
Methuselah	687	1656
Lamech	874	1651
Noah	1056	2006

Assuming there are no "gaps" in these chronological genealogies (a possibility which cannot be ruled out completely, but one for which there is no internal evidence), there seems to have been a total of 1656 years from the creation of Adam to the Flood. The recorded ages, however, are somewhat different in the Septuagint and other ancient versions, possibly because of copyists' errors in the numbers. Taking the ages at face value, it is interesting to note that Adam lived until Lamech, the father of Noah, was 56 years old. Most likely the oldest of the living patriarchs maintained the primary responsibility for preserving and promulgating God's

Word to his contemporaries. Since both Enoch and Lamech were outlived by their fathers, there were only seven men in the line before Noah who had this responsibility. This probably explains why, in II Peter 2:5, Noah is called "the eighth preacher of righteousness" in the "old world."

It is worth noting that the genealogies of Genesis 5 are repeated and thus confirmed as accepted by the later Biblical writers, both Old Testament and New Testament, in I Chronicles 1:1–4 and Luke 3:36–38.

Three facts seem to be emphasized in the record of the ten antediluvian patriarchs in Genesis 5: (1) God was preserving and recording the divinely-ordained line of the promised Seed, with the appropriate genealogical and chronological data; (2) God's command to "be fruitful and multiply" was being carried out, since the record recites that each one in the line "begat sons and daughters"; (3) God s curse was also in effect, since in spite of the fact each man lived many hundreds of years, eventually "he died."

The antediluvian line culminates in Noah (whose name means "rest") and his three sons, Shem, Ham and Japheth. At Noah's birth, his father Lamech prophesied of a coming time when the curse would be removed, indicating that the memory of the creation and fall was still fresh in the minds of at least those who had received and believed the records transmitted to them from Adam. Lamech (as well as Adam, Abel and Enoch) was undoubtedly one of those in Peter's mind when he spoke of "the times of restitution of all things, which God hath spoken by the mouth of all His holy prophets since the world began" (Acts 3:21). Noah, as the one who would by his Ark preserve life as the cursed earth was being "cleansed" by the waters of the Flood, was only a precursory fulfillment of Lamech's prophecy, of course. The promised Seed was still future, but in Him and His promised coming were true "rest" and "comfort."

The fact that Lamech spoke of the curse, and thus was evidently still keenly aware of the events in the Garden of Eden, is strong evidence that there cannot be any very large "gaps" in the genealogies of Genesis 5. It is impossible to postulate an age of a million or more years ago for man's beginnings, in conformity with the speculations of modern evolutionary anthropologists, and also to accept the records of Genesis 5 as historical and accurate.

Enoch and Lamech were themselves prophets of God, even though, in their time, they were under the primary authority of their fathers. A sample of Enoch's preaching is preserved in Jude 14, 15. Lamech's prophecy concerning the mission of his son Noah is recorded in Genesis 5:29.

Enoch's career is of special interest. He was one of only two men in history, the other being Elijah, who were caught up into Heaven without dying. In the midst of almost universal corruption and godlessness, Enoch bore a courageous and consistent witness to the men of his generation, and, as the Scripture says, he "was translated that he should not see death; ... for before his translation he had this testimony, that he pleased God" (Hebrews 11:5).

Enoch "walked with God" and was a prophet of God. As such, he preached against the godlessness of his generation in fearsome, thundering words: "Behold the Lord cometh with ten thousands of his saints (or "his holy myriads"), to execute judgment upon all, and to convince all that are ungodly among them of all their ungodly deeds which they have ungodly committed, and of all their hard speeches which ungodly sinners have spoken against him" (Jude 14, 15). It almost seems as though, when he spoke these words, he had Lamech particularly in mind.

The quotation in Jude seems to have been taken from one of three apocryphal books purportedly written by Enoch but actually dating from about the first century before Christ. These books contain much interesting material and, although most of it is surely fictional, it is possible that some actual traditions of Enoch's prophecies may have been handed down in the same manner as other records which eventually reached Moses and others. At least Jude, by divine inspiration, incorporated this particular fragment as of true Enochian authorship.

It is remarkable that Enoch would prophesy of the second coming of Christ even before the Flood, but this is clearly the meaning placed upon it by Jude. Actually, it may be considered as an amplification and exposition of the great prophecy of Genesis 3:15, the promise of the eventual crushing of the serpent, Satan, and his seed. God "left not himself without witness," even in the days of the antediluvians. The promised "coming" in judgment had a preliminary and precursory fulfillment in the great Flood, but its final fulfillment still awaits the glorious return and triumph of the Lord Jesus Christ.

Enoch's "walk" with God was, of course, not literal in the way that Adam had walked with Him in the garden before the Fall. Enoch shared the fallen nature of all men and thus could not physically even "look upon God and live." But "by faith," in prayer and by obedience to His word, he maintained close fellowship and communion with Him, a privilege equally possible to us today (Colossians 2:6; Galatians 5:16,25; II Corinthians 5:7). It is important to note that his walk with God was not such a mystical experience as to preclude a family life or a strong and vocal opposition to the unbelief and wickedness of his day.

The climax of Enoch's testimony was an event all but unique in history. "By faith Enoch was translated that he should not see death; and was not found, because God had translated him" (Hebrews 11:5). Nearly twenty-five centuries later, another prophet, Elijah was similarly taken into Heaven without dying (II Kings 2:11). It is significant that Enoch prophesied midway between Adam and Abraham, and Elijah midway between Abraham and Christ, and that both ministered in times of deep apostasy.

The translation of these two saints is perhaps a type of the promised translation of those who are trusting in Christ when He returns in the time of the end (I Thessalonians 4:16, 17). However, the two events are not strictly parallel, since the "rapture" of the saints is simultaneous with resurrection and glorification, and such an experience was impossible prior to the resurrection and glorification of Christ (I Corinthians 15:22, 23, 51–53).

There are also mentioned "two anointed ones that stand by the Lord of the whole earth" in Zechariah 4:14, and these in turn are connected with the "two witnesses" during the coming Tribulation period (Revelation 11:3, 4). These are to be slain when they have "finished their testimony," and then resurrected (Revelation 11:7–12) and translated. It is doubtful that one of these could be Moses, since Moses died once, and "it is appointed unto men *once* to die" (Hebrews 9:27). Enoch and Elijah have not yet died and Elijah, at least, is definitely to return to the earth to preach again (Malachi 4:5, 6; Matthew 17:11). It may well be, then, that this marvelous patriarch of old, Enoch will yet finish his ministry of witness to a godless generation, which was once cut short by his sudden translation while he walked with God.

Questions for Discussion

1. What does the record in Genesis 4 suggest about the state of technology in the antediluvian world?

2. Discuss the possible causes of the great ages of the antediluvian patriarchs.

3. Why do we find so few fossil remains of the pre-flood civilization?

4. Discuss the scientific evidences and problems of the canopy theory.

5. Where did Cain get his wife and the people to build and inhabit his city?

6. Discuss the unique testimony and career of Enoch, and his possible future ministry with Elijah.

7. How large could the world's population have become by the time of the flood?

Chapter 8

The Days of Noah

Genesis 6:1–7:16

The first age of human history was brought to its climax and culmination in the days of Noah. The sin-disease which began so innocuously when Eve was tempted to doubt the Word of God, which began to show the true ugliness of its character in the life of Cain and then came to maturity in the godless civilization developed by his descendants, finally descended into such a terrible morass of wickedness and corruption that only a global bath of water from the windows of Heaven could purge and cleanse the fevered earth. The characteristics of those awful and tragic days, strange as they may seem to our enlightened culture, are nevertheless to be repeated in the last days of the present age. It is thus important, from the standpoint of both past history and future guidance, that we understand the events that took place in the days of Noah.

Two days before Christ's crucifixion, His disciples asked Him, "What shall be the sign of thy coming, and of the end of the age?" (Matthew 24:3). His reply pointed to a number of "signs," all of which, occurring together in that generation (Matthew 24:34) would be *the* sign requested. The signs were climaxed with the warning, "But as the days of Noe were, so shall also the coming of the Son of man be. For as in the days that were before the flood, they were eating and drinking, marrying and giving in marriage, until the day that Noe entered into the ark, And knew not until the flood came and took them all away; so shall also the coming of the Son of man be"

(Matthew 24:37–39). Thus did Jesus not only verify the historicity of the Flood but also encourage us to study closely the characteristics of the days before the Flood.

Giants in the Earth (Genesis 6:1–13)

One of the most amazing facts revealed by paleontology (the study of fossilized remains of creatures which inhabited the earth in a former age) is that nearly all modern animals were once represented by larger ancestors. One thinks of the mammoths and cave bears, giant cockroaches and dragonflies and huge reptiles like the dinosaurs. Along with these are occasionally found fossilized giant human footprints, suggesting indeed that "there were giants in the earth in those days" (Genesis 6:4). Ancient traditions seem to recall a day when giants were known on the earth, and it is only a superficial sophistication which ignores the possibility that these may contain primitive reflections of the real events and characters described historically in the Genesis records.

Moral and spiritual conditions in the antediluvian world deteriorated with the passing years. Materialism and ungodliness abounded, except for the remnant connected with the line of the promised Seed and those few who may have been influenced by the witness of such men as Enoch.

Satan had not forgotten God's prophecy that a promised Seed of the woman would one day destroy him. He had implanted his own spiritual seed in Cain and his descendants, but God had preserved the line of the true Seed through Seth. When Noah was born and Lamech was led to prophesy that "comfort," concerning the Curse should come to the earth through him (Genesis 5:29), Satan and his angels must have feared that their opportunities for victory in the cosmic conflict were in imminent danger. Various explanations of Genesis 6:1–4 have been suggested by scholars, all of which are interesting. However, the following would seem most logical. Desiring reinforcements for a coming battle against the hosts of Heaven, they seem to have decided to utilize the marvelous power of procreation which God had given the human family and to corrupt it to their own ends. Men now were rapidly multiplying on the earth and by implanting their own seed in men, they could enlist in only one generation a vast multitude as allies against God. So these "sons of God saw the daughters of men ... and took them wives of all which they chose ... and they bare children unto them, the same became mighty men which were of old, men of renown" (Genesis 6:2, 4). This, they may have reasoned, would not only strengthen their own forces but might even succeed in corrupting the entire human race, destroying the integrity of the line of the promised Seed.

One's first reaction upon reading this passage is to think of the fairy tales of antiquity, the legends of ogres and dragons, and the myths of the gods consorting with men — and then to dismiss the entire story as legend and superstition. Christians have often been tempted to make the story more palatable intellectually by explaining the "sons of God" as Sethites and the "daughters of men" as Cainites, with the world's climax of wickedness developing as a result of breaking down the wall of separation between believers and unbelievers.

It is doubtless true that the families of the Sethites were eventually involved in all the worldliness and materialism of the Cainites, and that there probably were intermarriages — after all both groups were destroyed in the Flood. But such is certainly not the natural reading of the passage, and it does seem hard to understand why such an unnatural and unmitigated corruption should overtake the entire world merely because believers married unbelievers. The technical phrase "sons of God" is used elsewhere in the Old Testament *only* of angels (Job 1:6; 2:1; 38:7; Daniel 3:25). If the record refers merely to human marriages, it should more naturally have read "sons of Seth" and "daughters of Cain." After all, the sons of Seth were also "men" and "daughters of men" were born unto *them* too.

Perhaps the ancient legends of giants and of "demigods" have an element of true history preserved in them, even though later distorted and embellished by ages of oral transmission. The objection that angels could not beget children of human mothers presupposes more about angelic abilities than we know. Whenever angels have appeared visibly to men, as recorded in the Bible, they have appeared in physical bodies. Those who met with Abraham, for example, actually *ate* with him (Genesis 18:8).

On the other hand, a serious difficulty with this interpretation is the nature of the resulting progeny. How could any being actually be half-angel, half-human? What would be the potential spiritual destiny of such an individual? Fallen angels are irrevocably condemned, whereas unsaved men are at least potential subjects for redemption. The anomalous spiritual nature of such beings seems to preclude their existence. Nevertheless, the requirements of the text and context seem to require that the "sons of God" be understood as fallen angels, or demons, who somehow "took them women of all which they chose."

Most likely this stratagem was carried out by means of a technique akin to the demon-possession common in the times of Christ. The men whose bodies were possessed were evidently thereby made so attractive to women that they could take any they chose as wives. These "sons of God" thus controlled not only the men whose bodies they had acquired for their own usage, but also the wives they took to themselves, and then all the children they bore.

These children became the "giants," the mighty men of old. The word (Hebrew *nephilim*, meaning "fallen ones,") possibly gives a hint of the nature inherited from their pseudo-fathers, the fallen angels. The name came to mean "giants" and was applied later to the giants seen in Canaan by the Israelite spies (Numbers 13:33). By some means not known, these Satanically-controlled fathers were able to develop huge physical size in their offspring, and probably a monstrous desire for violence and destruction as well.

In any case, the "men of renown" resulting from these unions soon "filled the earth with violence"; the "wickedness of man was great in the earth," and "every imagination of the thoughts of his heart was only evil continually" (Genesis 6:4, 5, 11).

Such statements surely imply more than a *natural* state of sinfulness. This seems rather to be a *superhuman* calibre of wickedness, and thus is attributable mainly to Satan and his angels, who were still "sons of God" by creation, even though they had been disinherited.

The demoniacal combination of the materialism and ungodliness of the Cainitic civilization in general, with this irruption of the serpent's seed directly into large numbers of the human race and then with the thrusting forth of hordes of the monstrous offspring of these unlawful unions, all led to conditions in the world which were finally intolerable even to a God of compassion and longsuffering.

The corruption was so widespread and incurable that the only remedy was obliteration. Noah, the one righteous man of his generation, was finally told by God that, "I will destroy man with the earth" (Genesis 6: 13). Not only man and the animals, but the very earth on which they lived, would be destroyed by the coming Flood.

The intrigues of Satan and his angels quickly achieved astounding success, not only among the Cainites but even among the descendants of Seth. God had made man in His own image, to respond with a heart of love to God's love, but now "every imagination of the thoughts of his heart was only *evil* continually" (6:5). Man had been told to "multiply and fill the earth," but now "the earth was filled with *violence*" (6:11) and a state of anarchy and terror must have reigned. No wonder the Biblical writer, speaking from the human viewpoint said: "And it repented the Lord that he had made man on the earth, and it grieved him at his heart" (6:6).

But, for all his success, Satan was unable to touch one man (compare I John 5:18), and this was Noah, the one in the line of the promised Seed he would surely have desired to corrupt most of all! "But Noah found *grace* in the eyes of the Lord" (6:8).

What a wonderful word is *grace,* here appearing for the first time in Scripture! In sovereign mercy and by the election of grace, God prepared the heart of Noah to respond in obedient faith to His will.

Note the consistent Biblical order here (vv. 8 and 9). First, Noah "found grace." Then Noah was "a just man" (that is, "justified" or "declared to be righteous"); thus he was "perfect in his generations" (or "complete," in so far as God's records are concerned), and therefore he was able to "walk with God." Salvation in any era is exactly in this way. By sovereign grace, received through faith, the believer is justified before God and declared to be complete in Him. Only as a result of, and on the basis of, this glorious gift of grace, can one then "walk" in fellowship with God, showing the genuineness of his faith by his works. Four times it is said *later,* for example, that Noah "did all that God commanded him" (6:22; 7:5, 7:9; 7:16).

Warned of God (Genesis 6:14–7:16)

Just as world conditions in the days before the Flood presaged a coming catastrophe, so will world conditions in the last days of *this* age foreshadow an even greater catastrophe. This parallel is vividly set forth in the third chapter of II Peter which we shall see five chapters hence. For the present, we shall merely summarize here, without comment, some of the characteristics of Noah's day, because Christ said these would also characterize the days before His coming. Such a list could include the following: (1) preoccupation with physical appetites; (2) rapid advance in technology; (3) materialistic attitudes; (4) uniformitarian philosophies; (5) inordinate devotion to pleasure and comfort; (6) ungodliness in belief and conduct; (7) disregard for the sacredness of the marriage relation; (8) rejection of the inspired Word of God; (9) population explosion; (10) widespread violence and corruption; (11) preoccupation with illicit sex activity; (12) evidence of organized Satanic activity, manifest in abnormal depths of depravity of thought and conduct characterizing not only individuals but whole movements and systems. Each of the foregoing could, if space allowed, be supported both by specific Scriptures relating to the days of Noah and also by specific documentation relating to this present generation.

In order to preserve human and animal life on the earth, God instructed Noah to build a huge barge-like structure, called an ark, in which the occupants would be saved from destruction in the coming Flood. Only Noah and his family had resisted the corruption surrounding them. At the time of God's first announcement of the Flood, Noah's father and grandfather, Lamech and Methuselah, were still living, but Lamech died five years before it came, and Methuselah died in the very year of the Flood.

The Flood would be of such magnitude that it would destroy the earth itself (6:13), as well as all air-breathing creatures on the earth. The word for "Flood" (Hebrew *mabbul*) is only applied to the Noahic Flood; other floods are denoted by a different word in the original. *Mabbul* is related to an Assyrian word meaning "destruction"; the phrase "a flood of waters" (Genesis 6:17) could properly be translated by "a catastrophe of waters." Similarly, when the Genesis Flood is referred to in the New Testament, the Greek *kataklusmos* ("cataclysm") is uniquely employed.

According to God's instructions, the Ark was to be designed for floating stability and capacity rather than for moving through the sea. The dimensions were to be 300 cubits long, 50 cubits wide, and 30 cubits high. Assuming that the cubit was 17.5 inches in length (the exact value is uncertain, but this is the smallest number suggested by any of the authorities), the total volumetric capacity of the Ark was approximately 1,400 000 cubic feet, the same as that of 522 standard livestock cars such as used on modern American railroads.

A few other details of its construction are given. It had three stories, each ten cubits high, one window, probably extending all around the top, and one door in the side. It was made of gopher wood (the modern equivalent of which is unknown) and made waterproof with "pitch." It was fitted with "rooms" (literally "cells" or "nests") for the animals.

The word for "pitch" is different from that used in other places in the Old Testament. It means, simply, "covering" and is exactly the same as the Hebrew word for *atonement,* as in Leviticus 17:11. Whatever the exact substance may have been, it sufficed as a perfect covering for the Ark, to keep out the waters of judgment, just as the blood of the Lamb provides a perfect atonement for the soul.

According to God's statement to Noah (Genesis 6:17), the Flood would not only destroy mankind but also "all flesh, wherein is the breath of life, from under heaven." In order to "keep seed alive upon the face of all the earth" (7:9), Noah was instructed to take two of every kind of animal into the Ark with him, one male and one female. Of the "clean" animals (evidently those to be used for domestication and sacrifice), seven were to be taken aboard.

Most animals are small, of course, so this did not by any means represent an impossible task. Marine creatures were not to be included, as they could survive the flood waters. According to Genesis 7:22, "all that was in the dry land died." Authorities estimate that there are less than 18,000 species of mammals, birds, reptiles and amphibians in the world today. Even assuming that the biologic species is equivalent to the Genesis "kind" (in most cases, the "kind" was undoubtedly a unit of broader scope than this) and that the average species size is that of a sheep (undoubtedly much too large), one can quickly calculate that the Ark's capacity was abundantly large for its purpose. It is known that about 240 sheep can be transported in one stock car, so that 150 cars would suffice for 36,000 animals of this size. This is less than one-third the Ark's size. There was ample extra room for the approximately 1,000,000 species of insects, for food for possible animals now extinct, for living quarters for Noah and his family, and for any other necessary purposes.

The specifications which God established for the Ark were rigidly followed by Noah and thus the Ark was an extremely large and stable structure, perfectly designed for the tremendous function it would fulfill. The modern notion that the Flood was only a local or regional flood is refuted by this very fact — it was far too large for accommodating a mere regional fauna. In fact, no ark would have been necessary at all if the Flood were local. Not only the birds and mammals but also Noah and his family could have migrated to another country far more quickly and expeditiously.

It will be recalled that the climate before the Flood was probably uniformly warm all over the earth. Thus animals would not have been isolated in different latitudinal zones over the earth as at present, but probably each kind was found all over the world. No great distances were involved then, when the time came for representatives of each kind to migrate to the Ark.

The Lord told Noah that the animals would "come unto thee" at the proper time. To the selected animals, God must somehow have imparted a directional sense and an impelling urge to travel toward the one place of safety from the approaching storm. Only since the Flood have there been sharp latitudinal and seasonal temperature changes, and it seems possible that the present remarkable migratory and directional instincts possessed by animals, and especially by birds, could well have been inherited from their ancestors who came to the Ark.

Another remarkable physiologic mechanism possessed by most animals (possibly latent in all), as a protection against sharp temperature and other climatological changes, is the ability to suspend all bodily functions in a state of hibernation. There was no need for this ability before the meteorologic and climatologic changes caused by the Flood, so it is possible that this also was imparted to the animals on the Ark by God. One might think of divinely-ordered genetic mutations experienced by the individuals selected for preservation on the Ark, equipping them with the capacities for migration and hibernation. Then as they arrived at the Ark, and entered, and in response to the suddenly-darkened sky and the chill in the air, they settled down for a year-long "sleep" in their respective "nests" in the Ark.

The construction of the Ark and the other necessary preparations seems to have occupied 120 years (note Genesis 6:3) God announced, possibly through Methuselah or another of His prophets, as well as Noah, that His Spirit would only "strive with man" for another 120 years. Undoubtedly, Noah also spent much of this period preaching, warning men of the coming judgement (II Peter 2:5). But the uniformitarians of his day no doubt ridiculed such preaching. They had never seen a flood, or even rain, and the huge box Noah was building must have been a source of rich amusement to them. Their "science" had proved that a "flood of waters" was quite impossible, and so they went on "eating and drinking, marrying and giving in (possibly translatable as 'getting out of') marriage."

Until the Flood came! Noah had been warned of God "of things not seen as yet," and he preferred to believe the Word of God rather than the uniformitarian scientists of his day. Therefore he "prepared an ark to the saving of his house" (Hebrews 11:7).

"The Lord said to Noah: *Come* thou and all thy house into the ark; for thee have I seen righteous before me in this generation"

(Genesis 7:1). Because Noah exercised faith (Hebrews 11:7), God *saw* him as righteous, and saved both him *and his house.* This is God's gracious provision and promise to the one who is head of the house. "Believe on the Lord Jesus Christ and thou shalt be saved, and thy house" (Acts 16:31).

It is significant, too, that the Lord said, "Come," not "Go" (compare Matthew 11:28). This is the first occurrence of the word "come" in the Bible. God was in the Ark with them, and although the Flood would soon be unleashed in devastating fury, they were safe with Him.

All things were now ready. The animals had all been gathered into the ark, and food and other provisions stored on it. The ark was not only more than adequate in size to accommodate all known species of land animals, living or now extinct, but was also admirably designed to ride out the approaching storm in safety and comparative comfort. Both hydrodynamic calculations and laboratory wave-tank model testing have demonstrated that the ark was so dimensioned as to be exceedingly stable in the violent waters of the Flood. It was, once loaded, practically impossible to capsize, and would align itself in such a direction as to ride the waves most comfortably.

When all were safely inside and the Lord had shut the door, the Flood came. The windows (or "floodgates") of Heaven were opened and all the fountains of the great deep were broken up (literally, "cleaved open"). The vapor canopy above the firmament somehow condensed into great cloud banks, pouring forth torrents of waters without ceasing for forty days and nights. At the same time, the portion of the original "deep" (Genesis 1:2) which on the third day of Creation had evidently been entrapped beneath the crust, under high pressure, suddenly burst forth in great gushers through fissures opened up in the crust.

As the waters raged over the surface, gradually rising to destroy and bury the old world, the same waters bore the Ark and its occupants up far above the destruction experienced in the depths below. Thus the waters of judgment and death were also waters of cleansing and deliverance. In a "like figure" to this first great baptism, our baptismal waters now "save us" (I Peter 3:20, 21), setting forth in a most striking figure, the destruction of the old life and elevation to a new life, delivered from the bondage of corruption into the glorious liberty of the children of God.

Questions for Discussion

1. How are the days of Noah similar to those in which we live today, and does this indicate that Christ's return is near?

2. Discuss the different theories about the identity of the "sons of God" and the "daughters of men," and decide which is most likely.

3. Who were the "giants in the earth in those days," and what happened to them?

4. Discuss the references to Noah in the New Testament.

5. Show that the ark built by Noah was adequate to preserve all kinds of life on the earth.

6. How was it possible for Noah to gather animals from all over the world into the Ark?

7. How could Noah and his family take care of thousands of animals for a whole year in the Ark?

Chapter 9

The Flood and the Fossils

Genesis 7:17–8:14

In its long history, the earth has suffered much under the effects of the curse. Heat and cold, floods and droughts, earthquakes and eruptions — all kinds of physical upheavals — have disturbed its crust and the inhabitants dwelling on its surface. But immeasurably greater in magnitude and extent than all other physical catastrophes combined was the great Flood, which overwhelmed the earth in the days of Noah. In our modern age of science and skepticism the enormity of this great event of the past has been all but forgotten. Somehow its testimony to the awfulness of sin and the reality of divine retribution is so disturbingly unwelcome that men have sought at all costs to explain it away. Even conservative Christians, although professing belief in the divine inspiration of Scripture, have often ignored its significance.

As a matter of fact, the question of the nature and historicity of the Noahic Deluge is of immense importance to Biblical Christianity. The fact of the Flood is a pivotal issue in the entire conflict between Christianity and anti-Christianity. If the principle of innate evolutionary development can fully explain the universe and all its inhabitants, as its proponents claim, then there is no need to postulate a Creator. The chief evidence supporting evolution is the geological record of the supposed billions of years of earth history, documented by the fossils entombed in the sedimentary rocks of the earth's crust, and there is no room in this framework of interpretation for a world-destroying flood. Thus, if the latter has actually occurred, the assumptions of uniformity and evolution as guiding principles in interpreting earth history are thereby proved completely deceptive and false.

The Universal Deluge

In Noah's day, men scoffed at the warnings of the coming Flood; in our day men scoff at the record of the historical Flood. Nevertheless, as the Lord Jesus said: "The flood came, and destroyed them all" (Luke 17:27).

For over a hundred years, geologists and paleontologists have adhered to the principle of evolutionary uniformitarianism as the foundation of their interpretation of earth history. That is, they believe that all things should be explained in terms of slow growth and development over great ages by the operation of the same physical processes that now prevail. Accordingly, the concept of the universal Flood was completely rejected, and this led many Christians to attempt to work out a compromise between the Bible and evolutionary geology by explaining the Flood as a local flood, caused by a great overflow of the Euphrates or some other river in the Middle East. The first question to be settled, therefore, is whether or not the Biblical record describes a local or a universal flood.

The record of the Flood in Genesis gives every indication of being an eye-witness account, written originally by Noah or his sons. Despite the efforts of many commentators to explain it away as a local flood, it is obvious that the writer *intended* to tell of a worldwide, uniquely destructive cataclysm. In fact, it would be difficult to imagine how the concept of a universal Flood could be better presented than in the words actually recorded in Genesis.

In the first place, the skies poured down torrents of water continually for forty days and forty nights (Genesis 7:12, 17), which would be quite impossible under present meteorologic conditions. The only possible source for such a downpour would seem to be the condensation and precipitation of the antediluvian vapor canopy, the "waters above the firmament" of Genesis 1:7.

Then, as the waters increased and the Ark began to float, verse 18 says the water "prevailed," a word meaning literally "were overwhelmingly mighty." The next verse says they "prevailed exceedingly," until "all the high hills under the whole heaven were covered." And then the waters still rose until the mountains were covered — to a depth of at least fifteen cubits (verse 20). This depth was evidently the depth to which the Ark sank in the water, half its height, so that it could now float freely over the highest mountain tops.

The universality and totality of the Flood is further emphasized in verses 21–23, which stress the completeness of the destruction of all airbreathing creatures in the whole earth. "All in whose nostrils was the breath of life, of all that was in the dry land, died." Only those in the Ark were spared.

The conditions "prevailed" for a hundred and fifty days, with waters continuing to descend from the heavens and to issue from the great clefts in the earth's crust throughout this entire period, though perhaps not as steadily and torrentially as during the first forty days. Finally (Genesis 8:1–3), the fountains were stopped and the waters began to go down.

It is impossible to discuss here all the evidences supporting a worldwide Flood. In the writer's commentary *The Genesis Record* (Baker Book House, 1976, Appendix 5, pp. 683–686) are listed 100 distinct reasons why the Flood must be considered universal. The following are a few of the Biblical reasons:

(1) Expressions emphasizing universality of the Flood and its effects occur more that thirty times in Genesis 6 through 9.

(2) The wording of the record could not be improved on, if the intention of the writer were to describe a universal flood;

as a description of a river overflow, it is completely misleading and exaggerated, to say the least.

(3) The purpose of the Flood was to destroy man from she face of the earth (Genesis 6:7).

(4) The Flood was also intended to destroy all animal life on the dry land (Genesis 6:17; 7:22).

(5) The Flood was even to "destroy the earth" (Genesis 6:13).

(6) The waters covered all the mountains (Genesis 7:19, 20).

(7) The Flood was caused by a continual downpour lasting for forty days (impossible under present conditions), concurrently with a bursting of great clefts in the crust, releasing "the fountains of the great deep" (Genesis 7:11; 8:2).

(8) The Flood lasted over a year (Genesis 7:11; 8:13).

(9) The Ark was constructed for the purposes of keeping "seed alive upon the face of all the earth" (Genesis 7:3).

(10) The Ark was far too large to accommodate a mere local or regional fauna (Genesis 6:15).

(11) The Ark was entirely unnecessary for Noah, the animals, and especially the birds, to escape from a mere river flood.

(12) God's promise (Genesis 8:21; 9:11, 15) never to send such a Flood again has been repeatedly broken if it were only a local or regional Flood.

(13) The ordinary Hebrew word for "flood" is never used in describing the Noahic Flood, which is uniquely called *mabbul,* meaning essentially "destructive catastrophe."

(14) The New Testament uses a unique term (*kataklusmos* or "cataclysm") for the Flood (Matthew 24:39; Luke 17:27; II Peter 2:5; 3:6) instead of the usual Greek word for "flood."

(15) Even after four months of receding flood waters, the dove sent out by Noah could find no dry land on which to light (Genesis 8:9).

(16) All the earth's dry land animals now living are descended from those preserved on the Ark (Genesis 8:17, 19; 9:10).

(17) All men in the world today are descendants of Noah's three sons (Genesis 9:1, 19).

(18) New cosmological conditions prevailed after the Flood, including distinct seasons (Genesis 8:22), the rainbow (implying changed meteorological conditions — Genesis 9:13–4), and enmity between man and the animals (Genesis 9:2).

(19) Later Biblical writers accepted the universal Flood (note Job 12:15; 22:16; Psalm 29:10; 104:6–9; Isaiah 54:9; I Peter 3:20; II Peter 2:5; 3:5, 6; Hebrews 11:7)

(20) The Lord Jesus Christ accepted the historicity and universality of the Flood, even making it the climactic sign and type of the coming worldwide judgment when He returns (Matthew 24:37–39; Luke 17:26, 27).

In view of all the above facts, not even one of which can be explained satisfactorily in terms of a local flood, it is clear that the Word of God teaches unequivocally that the Flood was worldwide in its extent and effects. We must therefore reinterpret the geological evidence, now commonly understood in terms of uniformity and evolution, to conform to the Biblical revelation. This is clearly the only course legitimately open to Bible-believing Christians.

Occasionally, critics say there was not enough water to cover the earth. There is an equivalent depth of water vapor in the present atmosphere of less than two inches and this would hardly suffice for such a catastrophe! But there is plenty of water in the present ocean basins if the topography were slightly redistributed. If the earth's crust were evened out to form a smooth ball, the waters in the oceans would cover it to a depth of nearly two miles! These oceans now contain, of course, the tremendous quantities of water that came up from "the fountains of the great deep" and down from "the windows of heaven" during the Flood.

In order for the lands to emerge from the waters, it is clear that a great "continental uplift" had to take place. That is, the continents had to rise and the ocean basins to be depressed on a tremendous scale. This event seems to be mentioned in Psalm 104:6–9 (A.S.V.), especially verse 8: "The mountains rose, the valleys sank down...."

The physical mechanisms which God used to bring about the great uplift are not known. The soils and other light materials of the dry land had been eroded and washed into the antediluvian seas. Similarly the ocean bed had been upheaved by the bursting open of "the fountains of the great deep." The subterranean reservoirs of water were emptied as the water escaped to the surface, leaving great empty caverns in the crust below the surface.

Such a condition was unstable and could not persist for long. The heavy materials beneath the old land surfaces perhaps eventually began to sink, squeezing laterally underneath the lighter sediments in the adjacent basins, pushing them up to form continents and mountain ranges. Thus to some extent the land and water areas of the antediluvian earth may have been interchanged by the Flood, except that the water areas are now much more extensive. Perhaps this is the meaning of Job 12:15, which says that, when God sent the waters forth, they "overturned the earth."

The trigger mechanism that upset the unstable equilibrium and set the uplifting forces into operation seems to have been a great worldwide storm of wind (Genesis 8:1), with attendant electrical phenomena (Psalm 104:7). The wind was probably caused by the strong difference of temperature between polar and equatorial regions, brought about by removal of the thermal vapor canopy. The resulting giant waves and piling up of waters possibly created just enough additional unbalance of forces to cause tectonic (deformations in the crust of the earth, or faulting) movements to begin. Once begun, they would continue until the present equilibrium between continental and oceanic areas had been attained.

As the waters went down, the Ark finally lodged securely upon one of the mountains of Ararat (same as the Biblical "Armenia"). Both ancient traditions and numerous reported modern sightings indicate that the Ark is still preserved in the ice cap near the summit of the gigantic mountain known even today as Mount Ararat, located adjacent to Russia and Iran in eastern Turkey. This mountain is an extinct volcanic cone, formed probably during the Flood itself, now towering majestically over the 3000-foot plain around it to a height of 17,000 feet at its crest. Though its continued preservation has not been conclusively documented as yet, there does exist much evidence that the Ark is still there, hidden most of the time beneath the mountain's icy covering.

It is interesting to note the recurring significance of the "seventeenth day" in the narrative of the Flood. In the seventeenth day of the second month, the Flood began (Genesis 7:11); on the seventeenth day of the seventh month, the Ark settled safely on the mountains of Ararat (8:4). Then on the seventeenth day of the eleventh month, nine months after the Flood began, the dove returned with the olive leaf, indicating that plant life, with the necessary food for man's physical life, once again was growing in the earth (8:5, 6, 10, 11).

This day thus became, in effect, the "resurrection day" for the earth, and especially for the Ark and those preserved in it through the earth's great baptism. It is no doubt significant, therefore, that the anniversary of this date, many centuries later, was the date on which Christ rose from the dead! The seventh month of the Jewish civil year later was made the first month of the religious year, and the passover was set for the fourteenth day of that month (Exodus 12:2). Christ, our Passover, was slain on that day, but then rose three days later, on the seventeenth day of the seventh month of the civil calendar!

Securely anchored on the earth again, Noah and the others needed only to wait until the waters receded enough for them to disembark. But this took yet another seven months, so that they were evidently in the Ark slightly over a year, probably 371 days altogether. As the time passed, the tops of nearby lower mountains came into view. Noah finally released a raven and a dove. The dove returned but the raven, a scavenger bird with no qualms about resting on unclean surfaces, stayed. A week later Noah sent out the dove again, which returned this time with a fresh olive leaf, indicating that seedlings or cuttings from the hardy olive tree were already beginning to grow again on the mountain sides. Finally, the ground was sufficiently dried for the occupants of the Ark to disembark.

Although the Flood was over, abnormal weather conditions (development of continental glaciers, great volcanic flows and earth movements, violent storms and floods, etc.) no doubt continued for many centuries, as the earth gradually adjusted to new physiologic and hydrologic balances.

Geological Implications of the Flood

Any field of science which deals with earth history, such as geology, paleontology, archaeology, etc., must give full consideration to the extensive effects of the Flood on the data with which they deal, if their interpretation of earth history is to be legitimate. For the most part, however, this requirement has been either rejected or ignored by modern earth scientists. Instead, their interpretation of earth history has been built around the *principle of uniformity,* which explicitly denies any great geological catastrophe such as the Flood, and assumes that all geological formations were land down by the ordinary processes of nature, acting at essentially the same rates as at present. On the basis of this assumption, the tremendous size of many deposits seems to have required millions of years for their formation. However, the very same deposits can usually be explained equally well or better in terms of catastrophic deposition resulting from the Flood.

The most important scientific implication of the Flood has to do with the fossils. The sedimentary rocks which comprise most of the earth's crust in continental areas, have been deposited in layers known as strata by settling out of moving water. This is why they are called sedimentary rocks. Contained in these sediments are the fossils, remains of animals which once lived on the earth. Many of these kinds of animals are now extinct and often (not always, by any means) they are found in a more or less regular order, with the simpler fossils in the lower strata and the larger and more complex fossils higher up. This set of phenomena has been interpreted to teach the gradual evolution of living forms from the simple to the complex over great ages of geological time. In fact, this is the most important line of evidence supporting the theory of organic evolution! The geologic ages supposedly represented by the respective strata are actually identified and classified by the types of fossils they contain.

But a serious and tragic fallacy is present in this interpretation. Fossils necessarily speak of death and these rocks contain literally multiplied millions of fossilized animals. Death in turn speaks of sin and judgment — "the wages of sin is death" — and according to Scripture there was no death in the world before Adam's sin and God's curse on the whole creation. The fossils must therefore have been buried *after* Adam's fall! This in turn means that only a catastrophic death and burial can explain most of them, and the only catastrophe adequate in scope, variety and intensity is the Genesis Flood. Thus the fossils, rightly interpreted, will be found not to be proof of a long history of development and evolution of the earth, but rather to be a testimony to the great power and righteous judgment of the sovereign God, manifest in unprecedented majesty when "the world that then was, being overflowed with water, perished" (II Peter 3:6).

That the geologic column and its fossils were mostly due to the Flood is supported by the following physical facts:

(1) The sedimentary rocks, which contain the fossils on which the supposed geologic ages are based, were by definition deposited originally out of moving water, after having been transported by the water from their source.

(2) Most geologic formations are of such character as to require natural forces operating far more intensively than is found in the modern world. Many sand and gravel deposits are of far greater size than could be produced by modern rivers; most igneous rock formations are infinitely greater than modern volcanoes could ever form; glacial deposits are far beyond the capability of present glaciers to produce; coal-bearing formations are so vast that they could never be formed from plant materials as grown in modern peat-bogs; the petroleum reservoirs are so extensive that there is still no satisfactory theory explaining the origin of oil; the great mountain ranges and other structural features of the present earth could never be formed from modern earth movements. The same is true for almost every type of geologic formation.

(3) The vast deposits of fossils testify unequivocally to rapid, catastrophic burial. Most fossils would never have been preserved otherwise, but would quickly have been destroyed by decay or scavengers. Yet there are many locations where thousands and even millions of fish, or reptiles, elephants and rhinoceroses, and all kinds of animals, lie entombed in the rocks.

(4) All the rivers and lakes of the world once carried much greater volumes of water than they do now, as indicated by the alluvial deposits in their flood plains, by old river terraces and other evidences. Similarly, the world's deserts all give evidence of former humidity and fertility.

(5) It becomes clear from a detailed study of the geologic formations that there was no worldwide time break in sedimentary deposition during the formation of the entire geologic

column. Since, as noted above, each individual formation was laid down rapidly, and since each formation is succeeded by another one above it somewhere without a time break, therefore the whole series was formed continuously and rapidly.

Although there are still some unresolved problems in the Flood interpretation of the geological strata, these are not nearly so numerous nor so difficult as the problems faced by the evolutionary-uniformitarian interpretation of these strata. For detailed study of these evidences and difficulties, see the writer's book *The Genesis Flood* (co-author, John C. Whitcomb, published by Presbyterian and Reformed Publishing Co., Philadelphia, 1961, 518 pages). Furthermore, not only do these great beds of rocks and fossils support the Biblical record of the Flood, but they also repudiate the theory of evolution. To appreciate this, we must explain briefly the evolutionary interpretation of these strata and the fallacies involved in this interpretation.

The geologic ages have been arranged in a supposed chronological order, as follows, beginning with the "oldest" of the fossil-bearing strata. Cambrian (containing trilobites and other simple marine organisms); Ordovician; Silurian; Devonian (the age of fishes); Mississippian; Pennsylvanian (first insects); Permian (many amphibians and early reptiles); Triassic (age of dinosaurs); Jurassic; Cretaceous; Tertiary (age of birds and mammals); and Quaternary (age of man). This fossil record is the only significant evidence in favor of the theory of organic evolution. All other evidences commonly cited (such as those of comparative anatomy, embryological resemblances, geographical distribution, genetic mutations, vestigial organs, etc.) are strictly circumstantial in nature and can be explained better in terms of creation by a common Designer, with subsequent variation within the fixed limits of the created "kinds." Hereditary changes producing truly new characteristics, as by mutations, are almost always deteriorative in nature.

Thus, if the fossiliferous deposits are mainly records of the Flood year, instead of millions of years of evolutionary struggle, the entire theory of evolution is bankrupt. There is little wonder, therefore, that the concept of the geological ages is defended with such fervor, and that "flood geology" is ridiculed or ignored.

One should recognize, too, that nowhere in the world does the so-called "geological column" actually occur. It is quite possible for any vertical sequence of the "ages" to exist in any given locality. Any age may be on the bottom, any on top, and any combination in between. The contained fossils — rather than vertical superposition or any other feature of the formation — constitute the controlling factor in the "age" assigned it. Thus the theory of evolution is *assumed* in building up the geologic column, and *then the latter is taken as the proof of the theory of evolution!*

But the fossils speak eloquently of *death,* and therefore they must have been deposited after Adam's fall and God's resultant curse on the earth. Thus, at least in most instances, the fossils must have been buried by the Flood. In any one locality, of course, there would be a definite tendency for similar kinds of animals to be buried at about the same level and for different kinds to be buried in order of increasing size and complexity. Simple marine organisms would be buried first then fishes, then amphibians, then reptiles, birds and mammals. This is in order of: (1) increasing elevation of natural habitat; (2) increasing hydrodynamic resistance to gravitational settling in the sediment-bearing waters; and (3) increasing ability to flee from the encroaching floodwaters. *This is exactly what is commonly found in the sedimentary rocks, but it has been misinterpreted to teach a gradual evolution through the ages.*

Thus, God's record in the rocks is not a testimony to evolution but rather to His sovereign power and judgment.

Questions for Discussion

1. Is there enough water in the earth to cover all the highest mountains? Explain.

2. Where did all the water go after the flood?

3. Discuss the fallacies in the local flood theory and the tranquil flood theory.

4. Discuss the Biblical evidences for a worldwide flood.

5. Discuss the scientific evidences for a worldwide flood.

6. Are there other written records of the flood in addition to that in the Bible? Where? How many?

7. What was the physical mechanism that caused the flood?

Chapter 10

The New World

Genesis 8:15–9:17

The world after the Flood was very different from the world
Noah and his family had known before the Flood. The Ark
had provided the bridge — seemingly fragile and easily demol-
ished, but actually impregnable and secure — from the old
cosmos through the terrible Cataclysm to the present cosmos.
The lands that once had teemed with animals and people and
lush vegetation now were barren and forbidding. The air which
formerly was warm and still now moved in stiff and sometimes
violent winds, and there was a chill on the mountain slope
where the Ark rested. Dark clouds rolling about the sky, which
had once been perpetually and pleasantly bright, seemed to
threaten more rains and another flood. But the earth had been
pruned of the wicked hordes that had made its physical beauty
only a mockery, and God had granted a gracious opportunity
for a new beginning for the children of Adam.

And yet, despite the vast judgment and the new beginning,
the age-long conflict in the heavens between God and Satan
was still going on and would continue to affect the human
race, with continued failure on the part of man, yet continued
grace and deliverance by God.

After the Flood (Genesis 8:15–9:4)

A year and seven days earlier, God had said to Noah: "Come thou and all thy house into the ark" (Genesis 7:1). But now He said: "Go forth of the ark, thou and thy wife, and thy sons and thy sons wives with thee" (8:16). In both commands, God was speaking as from a location *within* the ark. The Ark, of course, is a wonderful type of the Lord Jesus Christ, carrying us safely through the baptismal waters of purging and death to a new life in Him. And these two commands, not contradictory but complementary ("enter the ark" — "leave the ark"), strikingly remind us of two complementary commands of Christ. First, He says, "*Come* unto me all ye that labor and are heavy laden, and I will give you rest" (Matthew 11:28). This command, all the more meaningful when we remember that "rest" was the very meaning of Noah's prophetic name, is but the preparation for His great command: "*Go ye,* therefore, into all the world and preach the gospel to every creature" (Mark 16:15).

The animal occupants of the Ark, now awakened from their long rest in the Ark, were also brought forth, and instructed to "breed abundantly" and to "multiply upon the earth." They and their progeny gradually spread out from Ararat, undoubtedly migrating and multiplying over many generations, until they found environments suited to their particular natures and needs. The Scriptures are clear in insisting that "every beast, every creeping thing, and every fowl, and whatsoever creepeth upon the earth, after their kinds, went forth out of the ark" (8:19). All the earth's present dry-land animals, therefore are descendants of those that were once on the Ark.

In like manner, all the present nations and tribes of mankind are descended from Noah's family. "These are the three sons of Noah: and of them was the whole earth overspread" (Genesis 9:19).

The earth's physical features were vastly changed and many of its physical processes were modified in various ways. The present hydrologic cycle was gradually established, with the energy of the solar radiation serving to draw up water by evaporation from the oceans and then to move it inland by the winds, whence it can condense into clouds and fall to the ground as rain or snow, finally to run off through the rivers or ground water channels back to the ocean again. This present hydrologic cycle marvelously provides for the maintenance of life on the present earth, in many different ways. Its ministry is often mentioned in the Bible, and always with remarkable scientific accuracy (for example, note Psalm 33:7; 135:7; Ecclesiastes 1:6, 7; Job 26:8; 36:27, 28; Isaiah 55:10).

Some of the implied physical changes after the Flood are as follows: (1) the oceans were much more extensive, since they now contained all the Flood waters; (2) the thermal vapor blanket had been dissipated, so that strong temperature differentials were inaugurated; (3) mountain ranges uplifted after the Flood emphasized the more rugged topography of the post-diluvian continents; (4) winds and storms were possible for the first time, as well as rain and snow; (5) the environment was much more hostile to man, especially because of the harmful radiations from space no longer filtered out by the vapor canopy, resulting in gradual reduction in human longevity after the Flood; (6) tremendous glaciers, rivers and lakes existed, with the world only gradually approaching its present state of semi-aridity; (7) the lands were barren, until plant life could be re-established through the sprouting of seeds and cuttings buried near the surface.

Although the new hydrologic cycle would produce rains, and sometimes floods, God assured Noah that there would never again be a worldwide flood which would destroy all life on the land. In fact, He assured him that a regular order of nature, with a fixed sequence of seasons and a fixed cycle of day and night, would thenceforth prevail as long as the earth itself remained (Genesis 8:21, 22). Thus, that regularity of nature which modern scientists have formalized as their "principle of uniformity" was instituted by God after the Flood. The seasons, heat and cold, day and night, are of course now controlled primarily by the sun, which actually supplies all the energy for the earth's physical processes. The earth's orbital revolution about the sun, its axial rotation and inclination, and its marvelous atmosphere also help establish these constants of nature, which in turn control most other geological processes. Thus, the promised uniformity of the seasons and the diurnal (daily) cycle implies the essential uniformity of all other natural processes. It is, of course, only these present processes, with which modern science is able to deal.

With such a forbidding and unpromising scene before him, and with an apparently imminent danger that the great rains and upheavals might start again at any time, Noah quite properly turned his thoughts toward God. Ever since Eden, the way of access to God had been through the offering of an animal sacrifice, and Noah had taken one extra animal of each "clean" species on the ark for this purpose. He proceeded immediately to build an altar (the first actual mention of an altar in the Bible) and to offer up burnt offerings of every clean land animal and every clean bird.

These were sacrifices both of praise and propitiation. Noah gave thanksgiving both for their deliverance from the corruption of the antediluvian world and their preservation through the Flood and also made intercession for his descendants in the new world, that their lives might he protected and the earth not again destroyed. "And the Lord smelled a sweet savour ..." that is, He heard and respected the believing, though perhaps unspoken, prayer of Noah, represented by the incense rising from the smoke of the burnt offering. All the remaining verses of this section are taken up with God's gracious answer to Noah's prayer.

He first of all relieved their apprehensions by promising never again to destroy all life on the earth, smiting the earth with such a devastating curse as it had just experienced (the curse of Genesis 8:21 is obviously the Flood, not the Curse of

Genesis 3:17 which will prevail until the new earth of Revelation 22:3 is created). His reason for this promise seems
strange: "...for the imagination of man's heart is evil from his
youth." This would seem at first to be justification for smiting
the earth, rather than for promising not to do so, until we
remember again the great paradox of the grace and love of
God. Here is a testimony both to what theologians call original
sin and universal depravity and yet also to God's redeeming
mercy. Because man is helpless to save himself, his very
thoughts born and nurtured in sin, he desperately needs the
grace of God. On the basis of an atoning sacrifice, God's
salvation and blessing are received by simple faith. Thus, for
the very reason that man is completely unable to save himself,
therefore God saves him! Truly, He is the God of all grace!

After promising the essential uniformity of earth processes
in the future, God then instructed Noah, as He had Adam in
the beginning to "be fruitful and multiply and fill the earth."
Possibly the omission here of a renewal of the command to
"have dominion over the earth and subdue it" (Genesis 1:28)
is intimation that, despite the destruction of many of his hosts
in the Flood, Satan still retained at least proximate dominion
on the earth (1 John 5: 19). On the other hand, since the original
command to Adam was not rescinded at this time, its intent
has not changed and is still basically in effect, though its
implementation is hindered because of sin in human life.

Thus man no longer was to exercise a gentle authority over
the animal creation; there was to be fear manifest by the
animals, rather than obedience and understanding. Furthermore, animals were for the first time authorized for use as
food (although quite likely this had been done before the Flood
without authorization). The reason for this change is not obvious; perhaps the more rigorous environment in the new world
required the protein in meats for man's sustenance, to a degree
not available in other foods. Possibly the Lord also designed
this to show the great gulf between man and the animals,
anticipating the dangers implicit in the evil doctrine of the

evolutionary continuity of life of all flesh, which ultimately equates man with the animals and denies the Creator, in whose image man alone was made.

But with this permission, there was also the restriction: "... flesh with the life thereof, which is the blood thereof, shall ye not eat." The flesh of the animal was given for meat, but the *life* of the flesh was given for sacrifice. "For the life of the flesh is in the blood; and I have given it to you upon the altar to make an atonement for your souls: for it is the blood that maketh an atonement for the soul" (Leviticus 17:11). The words "life" and "soul" in these verses are the same word (Hebrew *nephesh*). The blood of course performs the physiological function of conveying the necessary chemicals from the food and air to sustain and renew the physical flesh, and particularly to maintain the consciousness and the orderly thought-process of the brain. All of this complex of marvelous operations is called the "life" or the "soul," the self-consciousness which distinguishes animal life from plant life. The "life" of a clean animal, spilled upon a sacrificial altar, was accepted by God in substitutionary death for the life of a guilty sinner, who deserved to die but who was permitted to live because of the sacrifice, whose blood "covered" his sins.

The Noahic Covenant (Genesis 9:5–17)

The blood of animals could only figuratively cover sins, of course. The reality represented by the figure was the sacrifice of the Lamb of God, Jesus Christ, who "now once in the end of the world hath appeared to put away sin by the sacrifice of himself" (Hebrews 9:26).

Thus the blood of animals, repressing their life, was sacred and not to be eaten, since it was accepted in sacrifice in substitution for the life of man. Man's blood in turn, representing *his* life, was yet more sacred, for "in the image of God made he man" (Genesis 9:6). Though animals shared the possession of a soul and body with man, it was only man who had an eternal spirit, the image of God.

Neither beast nor man was therefore permitted to spill man's blood. From any animal or any man who shed human blood, God would require satisfaction, and that would be nothing less than the very blood of their own lives (9:5).

The authority to execute this judgment of God upon a murderer was then delegated to man. "Whoso sheddeth man's blood, by man shall his blood be shed: for in the image of God made he man," (Genesis 9:6). The anarchistic conditions that had developed before the Flood — men slaying whom they would and defending themselves as they could — were not to be permitted to recur.

Thus was instituted the system of human government. The power thus given over man's life surely implies also power over all lesser categories. The instruction here given in no way refers merely to vengeance; the emphasis is rather on justice and on careful recognition of the sacredness of the divine image in man, marred by sin though it be. Obviously some means for impartial verification of guilt prior to execution of the judgment is assumed, though no formal legal system is here outlined. Evidently the particular form of government might vary with time and place, but the *fact* of human government exercised under God, is clearly established.

Thus the so-called "dominion mandate" given by God to Adam in the beginning (Genesis 1:26 — 28) was renewed in modified form to Noah. Both Adam and Noah were to multiply and fill the earth and (except for Satanic interference) to have dominion over all the earth and even over its animal population. The mandate was expanded now, however. Not only must man control the animals, he must now govern himself and his societies. In return, God would establish a new covenant with mankind and all creatures of the earth. This Noahic covenant thus embraces and enlarges the original Adamic dominion mandate, to include particularly the institution of human government, as epitomized in the responsibility of capital punishment.

Before the Flood, there apparently had been no formal mechanism for punishment or crime prevention, even for the capital crime of murder, as evident in the histories of Cain and Lamech. Evidently each individual was able to act quite independently of all restraints except those of his own conscience and self-interest. This eventually led to a universal state of violence and anarchy. To prevent the development of similar conditions after the Flood, God established the institution of human government.

It is clear that the authority for capital punishment implies also the authority to establish laws governing those human activities and personal relationships which, if unregulated, might eventually lead to murder. Thus this simple instruction to Noah is the basis for all human legal and governmental institutions.

The modern "liberal" objections to capital punishment are insufficient to warrant setting aside this decree of God. The prohibition in the Ten Commandments against killing plainly applies only to murder, not to judicial executions; in fact, the Mosaic laws themselves established capital punishment as the penalty not only for murder but also for breaking *any* of the ten commandments (note Hebrews 10:28).

Similarly, the Christian dispensation in no way sets aside these provisions of the Noahic covenant. The eating of meat (I Timothy 4:3, 4), the abstinence from blood (Acts 15:19, 20), and the authority of the governmental "sword" (Romans 13:4) are all re-affirmed in the New Testament. Christ, in fact, seemed almost to echo God's words to Noah, when He said: "...all they that take the sword shall perish with the sword." (Matthew 26:52).

As is evident from these passages, as well as from such Scriptures as I Peter 2:13–17; Acts 25:10,11; Romans 13:1–7, and others, it is evident that these provisions of the Noahic covenant are still in force among all nations as far as God is concerned. He is even today controlling the social order through the instrumentality of human government, first ordained through Noah after the Flood.

The Hebrew word *shaphak* is most interesting. It is translated "sheddeth" in Genesis 9:6, where it is used in the Bible for the first time. It is often translated also as "poured out" or "poured forth" or "shed forth." It is frequently used of the "pouring out" of the wrath of God (for example, Psalm 69:24), but also of the pouring out of His Spirit (Joel 2:28). Many times it refers to the pouring out of the blood of the animal sacrifices at the base of the altar (for example, Leviticus 4:30). It is the word used prophetically by Christ on the cross when He cried: "I am poured out like water" (Psalm 22:14).

Its first mention, here in Genesis 9:6, thus stresses not only the sacredness of human life, but also points us forward to the One who was most perfectly and eternally "in the image of God," and Whose blood would be shed judicially, though utterly unjustly by human governmental authority — but Who, in the marvelous counsels of God, thereby "made his soul an offering for sin" (Isaiah 59:10).

For a "token of the covenant" God established the beautiful rainbow in the clouds. Just as the fossil-bearing rocks of the earth's crust should continually remind us that God once destroyed the earth with a Flood, so the rainbow after the rain should remind us that He will never do so again. In fact, regardless of the latter-day threats of thermonuclear bombs, death rays, germ warfare, and the like, we have His promise that at least until the end of the millennium — "while the earth remaineth," He will not again "smite any more everything living" (Genesis 8:21, 22).

The "bow in the cloud" (9:13), of course, requires both sunlight and "the cloud" — that is liquid water droplets in the air — before it can form. Before the Flood, the upper air contained only invisible water *vapor,* and therefore no rainbow was possible. With the present hydrological cycle, the former vapor canopy is gone, and it is physically impossible now for enough water ever to be raised into the atmosphere to cause a universal Flood. When a storm has done its worst and the clouds are finally exhausted of most of their water, then there always appears a rainbow, and God would have us remember once again His promise after the great Flood.

The rainbow thus demonstrates most gloriously the grace of God. The pure white light from the unapproachable holiness of His throne (Timothy 6:16) is refracted, as it were, through the glory-clouds surrounding His presence (I Kings 8:10, 11) breaking into all the glorious colors of God's creation. In wrath He remembers mercy. The glory follows the sufferings, and where sin abounded, grace did much more abound!

The rainbow reappears only three more times in Scripture. Once, in Ezekiel 1:28, the rainbow is seen surrounding the throne of God as He prepares to visit judgment upon His people Israel. Again, the rainbow is seen around His throne just before the coming Great Tribulation, in Revelation 4:3. Finally, the mighty angel of Revelation 10:1, none other than the Lord Jesus Christ Himself, comes to claim dominion over the world. And instead of a crown of thorns, which once He wore as He bore the Curse for us, the Word says there will be "the rainbow upon His head." Forevermore, it is thus that we shall see our Lord Jesus *crowned* with glory and honour; that he by the grace of God should taste death for every man" (Hebrews 2:9).

Questions for Discussion

1. In what ways was the post-flood world different in physical aspect from the pre-flood world?

2. How did the animals get from Mount Ararat to all the continents (e.g., the kangaroo and koala to Australia)?

3. Why did God arrange for the Ark to come to rest on Mount Ararat instead of, say, Mount Mckinley, or somewhere else?

4. Discuss the evidence that the Ark may still be preserved high up on Mount Ararat.

5. What evidences of the flood can we still see in the present structure of the earth's surface?

6. Why did Noah have seven of each "clean" kind of animal on the Ark, and only two of the others?

7. Discuss the cause and significance of rainbows, and the places where they are mentioned in the Bible.

Chapter 11

Origins of Races and Nations

Genesis 9:18–10:32

The race question is certainly one of the most important and explosive issues of our time, and the same is true for the issue of nationalism versus internationalism. The existence of distinctive "races" and nations and languages is obviously a fact of modern life, in spite of the efforts of many modern sociologists and politicians to remove racial and national barriers. The problems created by these issues seem almost insurmountable. The true origin of the world's various races and nations and the events associated therewith must be clearly understood and placed in right perspective before there is any possibility that the problems rising out of them can be comprehended and solved.

In the world today there seem to be several major "races" (three to six, depending upon the particular classification) perhaps 100 or more nations of significance, and over 3000 tribal languages and dialects. And yet all of this diversity of peoples and tongues must have come from a common ancestor, because all of these are true men, capable of physical inter-relationships, capable of learning and education, and even capable of spiritual fellowship with the Creator, through faith in Christ. The origin of races and nations is still a mystery to most scientists, determined as they are to explain man and his culture in terms of an evolutionary framework. There are numerous contradictory theories on these matters among anthropologists and ethnologists, but the only fully reliable record of the origin of races, nations and languages is found here in Genesis 9 through 11.

The Threefold Division of Mankind
(Genesis 9: 18–29)

The Scriptures are explicit in teaching that all men now living in the world are descended from Noah through his three sons, Shem, Ham and Japheth (note Genesis 9:19; 10:32; Acts 17:26). All the physical characteristics of the different nations and tribes must have been present in the genetic constitutions of the six people who came through the Flood in the Ark. By the regular mechanisms of genetics — variation, segregation, etc. — supplemented by mutations in some instances, the various groups of nations developed.

It is significant that the Bible never mentions race at all; neither the word nor the concept is found in Scripture. A race, in evolutionary terminology, is a sub-species evolving into a new species but, in reality, there is no such thing. That is, as far as mankind is concerned, there is only one race — the human race. The various divisions are those of nations, tribes and languages — not races. Nevertheless, there have been three major groups of nations in world history, and these are those originally established by the three sons of Noah.

According to Acts 17:26, God had a specific time and place and purpose for each nation. Although each tribe and nation was to contribute to the corporate life of mankind as a whole, the overriding purpose of every national entity was "that they should seek the Lord" (Acts 17:27).

The basic outline of the function of each of the three major groups is given in the remarkable prophecy of Noah in Genesis 9:25–27.

It is significant that, as the great prophecy of Genesis 3:15 was given as a result of the fall of Adam, this prophecy was given as a result of the fall of Noah.

The parallel between the two situations is striking. Both Adam and Noah were commanded to fill the earth and to exercise control over it. Each of them is actually the ancestor of all men in the present world. Each sinned by partaking of a fruit, Noah of the fruit of the vine and Adam of the fruit of the tree of knowledge. As a result, each became naked and then each was provided with a covering by someone else. Finally the prophecy resulting in each case included a curse which has affected mankind ever since.

The Adamic nature was of course still a part of the Noahic heredity, and this fact, coupled with the terrible moral environment of the antediluvian world, was bound to leave Noah and his sons still subject to Satanic temptation. Ham, especially, seems to have been secretly rebellious and carnally minded. The tragic story of Noah s drunkenness and the sudden unveiling of Ham's rebellious heart provides graphic evidence that, despite the cleansing judgment of the Flood, man was still a sinner and Satan still "the spirit that now worketh in the sons of disobedience" (Ephesians 2:2). But the behavior of Shem and Japheth, as well as that of Ham, in this time of sudden family crisis provides the clue to their characters and the occasion for Noah's remarkable prophecy.

The principle of first mention is at axiom of Bible study which has been verified in a great number of instances. Despite its variety, the Bible is a wonderful unity, with every part perfectly consistent with every other part. Thus when any important word is mentioned in the Bible for the first time the circumstances and usage of the word at that point establish the predominant theme around which it will later be developed all through Scripture.

Thus the first time "wine" is mentioned in the Bible, it occurs in connection with the drunkenness and shame of Noah.

Undoubtedly the nature of wine was well-known to the ante-diluvians, and there is no intimation in the Scriptures that Noah was not fully cognizant of what he was doing when he made and drank his wine. The Scriptures do not hesitate to call attention to the failures of even the saintliest of men. Noah, having stood strong against the attacks of evil men for hundreds of years, remaining steadfast in the face of such opposition and discouragement as few men have ever faced, now let down his guard, as it were, when it seemed that all would be peace and victory henceforth. After all he had been through, what harm could there be in a little relaxation and a little provision for the desires of the flesh?

But the Scriptures warn: "Be sober, be vigilant; because your adversary the devil, as a roaring lion, walketh about, seeking whom he may devour" (I Peter 5:8). Satan had been unable to corrupt the family of Noah before the Flood, although he had succeeded with all other families and he now seized his opportunity. The formation of intoxicating wine from the pure, healthful juice of grapes is a perfect symbol of corruption and decay. The process of fermentation is a decay process and the effect of drinking the alcoholic product of this decay is likewise, in several respects, a "breaking down," both physically and morally. It is essentially the same process as that of "leavening," which is everywhere in Scripture symbolic of corruption.

Noah doubtless had no intention of drinking to excess, but he did. The artificial heat induced by the wine impelled him to throw off his clothing and finally he sprawled in a drunken sleep in his tent, where his son Ham saw him. The word "saw" implies "gazed at," evidently with satisfaction. Most likely, there was a carnal and rebellious bent to Ham's nature, thus far restrained by the moral strength and authority of his father. Now, beholding the evidence of his father's own human weakness before his very eyes, he rejoiced, no doubt feeling a sense of release from all the influences which had heretofore inhibited his own desires.

Thinking his brothers would share his satisfaction, he hastened to tell them the savory news. But they responded quite differently, refusing even to look on their father's shame and doing instead what they could to help him, covering him with the garment he had discarded.

When Noah finally wakened, he must have noticed the robe placed on him and then inquired until he learned what had transpired. As ashamed as he must have been of his own moral lapse, he realized that the sin of Ham was far greater, since it revealed a heart of rebellion and unbelief, not only against his father, but also against his father's God. Similarly, the act of Shem and Japheth plainly testified of their own reverential faith in the Lord.

With the deepest hearts of his own sons thus laid bare before him, Noah was moved to make the great prophetic declaration of Genesis 9:25–27. To some extent the insight thus revealed into the future was no doubt based on the insight he had into the hearts of his sons. Knowing them, and their children, he could foresee the future course their descendants would follow. But, more importantly, he spoke in the Spirit, prophesying as the Spirit gave utterance.

Although Noah's declaration (Genesis 9:25–27) does involve a curse on Ham's posterity and a blessing on Shem and Japheth, it is to be regarded as a prophecy rather than an invocation. Noah was predicting, not praying, and the prediction was undoubtedly premised on the characters revealed by his sons.

The Scripture says that "God has made of *one* all nations of men." Thus, in spite of the threefold division into Semites, Hamites and Japhethites, all mankind is a unity. And whenever one encounters a fundamental threefold unity (such as seen almost everywhere in the physical universe, and in the nature of man himself, as noted earlier), one almost inevitably thinks of the divine Trinity.

All people are basically threefold in nature — body, soul and spirit — (I Thessalonians 5:23), referring to their physical, intellectual and spiritual natures, respectively. However, each person is dominated by one of the three. Some people are concerned mainly with physical motivations, others with mental activities, and the rest with religious pursuits. The same applies to nations, and this seems to have been the main thrust of Noah's prophecy. As he knew the characters of his own sons, he could foresee that their respective descendants would be characterized chiefly by religious zeal (Shem), mental acumen (Japheth) and materialistic drives (Ham).

Though he could gladly pronounce a blessing upon his sons Shem and Japheth, he could not bring himself to pronounce a curse directly on his other son, Ham, though he knew prophetically that such a curse would be the lot of his descendants. Thus he said instead, as it were: "Cursed *is* (not 'be') Canaan since he, along with his older brothers, has inherited the rebellious and carnal nature of his father Ham. Their future will be one of service — providing mainly for the material and physical needs of mankind. Shem, on the other hand, with his concern for the Lord and His honor, will through his descendants lead men to know and follow God. Japheth also, with his more serious approach to life and its meaning, will see his descendants enlarged geographically and mentally, coming to dwell finally in the spiritual house built by the children of Shem. The children of Ham, however, even those of his youngest and least responsible son, Canaan, will have to be content with giving service to both Shem and Japheth providing the material basis of human society, upon which the spiritual and intellectual concerns of mankind can be superposed."

As far as the fulfillment of the prophecy is concerned, it has taken place in both a genuine and a counterfeit sense, manifesting the continued conflict between the spiritual seed of the woman and the seed of the serpent, both of which exist in all three "races" of mankind. From the descendants of Shem, for example, have come the Hebrews, through whom God gave the Scriptures and "of whom as concerning the flesh Christ came" (Romans 9:5). On the other hand, from other Semites, have come false religions, such as Islam. Most of the major features of all forms of paganism, whether in ancient or modern religions, came originally from the religions of the Babylonian and Assyrian Semites.

The descendants of Ham were marked especially for secular service to mankind. Indeed, they were to be "servants of servants," that is "servants *extraordinary!*" Although only Canaan is mentioned specifically (possibly because the branch of Ham's family through Canaan would later come into most direct contact with Israel), the whole family of Ham is in view. The prophecy is worldwide in scope and, since Shem and Japheth are covered, all Ham's descendants must be also. These include all nations which are neither Semitic nor Japhetic. Thus, all of the earth's "colored" races, — yellow, red, brown, and black — essentially the Afro-Asian group of peoples, including the American Indians — are possibly Hamitic in origin and included within the scope of the Canaanitic prophecy, as well as the Egyptians, Sumerians, Hittites, and Phoenicians of antiquity.

The Hamites have been the great "servants" of mankind in the following ways, among many others: (1) they were the original explorers and settlers of practically all parts of the world, following the dispersion at Babel; (2) they were the first cultivators of most of the basic food staples of the world, such as potatoes, corn, beans, cereals, and others, as well as the first ones to domesticate most animals; (3) they developed most of the basic types of structural forms and building tools and materials; (4) they were the first to develop fabrics for clothing and various sewing and weaving devices; (5) they were the discoverers and inventors of an amazingly wide variety of medicines and surgical practices and instruments; (6) most of the concepts of basic mathematics, including algebra, geometry, and trigonometry were developed by

Hamites; (7) the machinery of commerce and trade — money, banks, postal systems, etc. — were invented by them; (8) they developed paper, ink, block printing, movable type, and other accoutrements of writing and communication. It seems that almost no matter what the particular device or principle or system may be, if one traces back far enough, he will find that it originated with the Sumerians or Egyptians or early Chinese or some other Hamitic people. Truly they have been the "servants" of mankind in a most amazing way.

Yet the prophecy again has its obverse side. Somehow they have only gone so far and no farther. The Japhethites and Semites have, sooner or later, taken over their territories, and their inventions, and then developed them and utilized them for their own enlargement. Often the Hamites, especially the Negroes, have become actual personal servants or even slaves to the others. Possessed of a genetic character concerned mainly with mundane matters, they have eventually been displaced by the intellectual and philosophical acumen of the Japhethites and the religious zeal of the Semites.

The Japhethites have been "enlarged," taking over lands originally settled by Hamites, and developing the Hamitic technology into *science* and *philosophy*. Japhethites have provided the intellectual aspect to humanity's life, Hamites the physical and Semites the spiritual. Japheth has, even in the present age, largely taken over the religious function from Shem — "dwelling in the tents of Shem."

These very general and broad national and racial characteristics obviously admit of many exceptions on an individual genetic basis. It is also obvious that the prophecy is a divine description of future facts, in no way needing the deliberate assistance of man for its accomplishment. Neither Negroes nor any other Hamitic people were intended to be forcibly subjugated on the basis of this Noahic declaration. The prophecy would be inevitably fulfilled because of the innate natures of the three genetic stocks, not by virtue of any artificial constraints imposed by man.

The Table of Nations (Genesis 10:1–32)

Even higher critics have often admitted that the tenth chapter of Genesis is a remarkably accurate historical document. Here is the link between the historic nations of antiquity and the prehistoric times of Noah and the antediluvians. The grandsons and great-grandsons of Noah are listed, each of whom is identified with the city or country established by his descendants.

The earliest descendants of the sons of Noah, whose names were originally essentially synonymous with the tribes or nations which they founded, are given in this fascinating document known as the Table of Nations. There is nothing in all the ancient writings discovered by archaeologists which is at all comparable in scope and accuracy. It gives every appearance of being a sort of family record, kept by a venerable patriarch of the family as long as he remained alive and could keep in touch with his descendants.

Shem, as the oldest son and also as the one most interested in God's promise of the coming Seed, would be the logical one to keep such a record. He lived for 502 years after the Flood (Genesis 11:10, 11), which would have encompassed the entire period included in the Table of Nations. It is significant that the sons of Ham and Japheth are given only to the third generation after the Flood, whereas Shem's descendants extend to the sixth, indicating perhaps that he lost touch with the other branches of the family after the Dispersion. His signature is attached in the subscript at Genesis 11:10, after he had written of the events at Babel.

It has been possible in most cases to identify the names in Genesis 10 with nations and peoples known to archaeology. Thus it provides the link between recorded history and the period of "pre-history" which is, except for the Biblical records, preserved only in ancient traditions.

It is possible, for example, to trace the names of the sons of Japheth, allowing for the gradual modifications in structure that always occur in such names with the passage of time, and to recognize the ancestors of most of the Indo-European group of peoples. Space does not permit citing the evidence, but it is believed there is support for the following identifications (secular historical name in parentheses): Japheth (Iapetos, the legendary father of the Greeks and Iyapeti, the reputed ancestor of the Aryans in India); Gomer (Cimmeria, Crimea, Germany, etc.); Ashkenaz (Scandinavia, Saxony); Riphath (Paphlagonia, Carpathia); Togarmah (Armenia); Magog (meaning "place of Gog," therefore Georgia); Meschech (Moscow); Tubal (Tobolsk); Madai (Media); Javan (Ionia); Elishah (Hellas); Tarshish (Tartessos, Carthage); Kittim (another name for Cyprus; also, when combined with the prefix "ma," Macedonia); Dodanim (Dardanelles, Rhodes); Tiras (Thrace).

In similar fashion the sons of Ham seem to have the following identifications: Cush (Ethiopia); Mizraim (Egypt); Phut (Libya); Canaan (Palestine). The original names disappeared, but these identifications are supported by numerous Biblical and secular references. Some of the grandsons' names seem to have been preserved as follows: Ludim (Lydia); Heth (Hittites, — possibly Khittae and Cathay); Sin (Sinite, possibly Sinai, and even China); Resen (Etruscan); Nimrod (Merodach, the chief deity of Babylonia).

Among the children of Shem, the following are reasonable identifications: Elam (Elamites, the ancient Persians); Asshur (Assyria); Peleg (Pelasgians); Aram (Aramaeans, or Syrians); Eber (Hebrews, Ebla). The sons of Joktan were all identified with the Arabian peninsula.

Some of the foregoing identifications, as well as others that could be mentioned, may be doubtful, but there is surely enough evidence to warrant the general correlation of Shem,

Ham and Japheth with the Semitic nations, Afro-Asian nations and Indo-European nations, respectively.

One remarkable feature of the Table of Nations will be noted in closing. There are exactly seventy of the "families of the sons of Noah" mentioned, and it was "by these that the nations were divided in the earth after the flood" (Genesis 10:32). This is the same as the number of the children of Israel which came into Egypt from Canaan (Genesis 46:27). Later (Deuteronomy 10:22), when Israel had multiplied and was returning out of Egypt and was itself to become a nation — in fact, God's chosen nation — Moses exhorted the people to "remember the days of old ... when the Most High divided to the nations their inheritance, when he separated the sons of Adam, he set the bounds of the people according to the number of the children of Israel" (Deuteronomy 32:7, 8).

This number "seventy" has ever since been peculiarly identified with the nation Israel. Thus "seventy weeks were determined upon thy people" (Daniel 9:24), and Israel's history can be understood within a remarkable framework of successive cycles of seventy "weeks" of years. Israel was led by seventy elders (Numbers 11:16, 25) and later there were seventy members of the Jewish Sanhedrin. Seventy scholars translated the Old Testament into Greek to produce the Septuagint version of the Scriptures. Moses also wrote that man's allotted lifespan was seventy years (Psalm 90:10). The Babylonian captivity of Israel lasted seventy years.

By all these "families of the sons of Noah" were the nations "divided in the earth after the flood" (Genesis 10:32). The division actually took place after the confusion of tongues at the Tower of Babel (note the reference to different "tongues" in Genesis 10:5, 20, 31). The respective families of nations then, each in their respective ways, were ordained to implement the prophecy of Noah (9:25–27) thus making their contribution to human society as a whole. Finally, all nations alike were to "be fruitful and multiply," maintaining law and order under God (Genesis 9:6, 7), with the purpose that they all might "seek the Lord" (Acts 17:27).

Questions for Discussion

1. Discuss the biological meaning of the "race" concept, and the significance of the fact that the concept of race is not found in Scripture.

2. What are some of the contributions of the Hamitic nations to human civilization?

3. Does the curse on Canaan justify slavery or racism, as some have claimed? Why, or why not?

4. What have been the chief contributions of the Semitic and Japhetic nations?

5. Is the use of wine or other intoxicating drinks appropriate or inappropriate for Christians?

6. Is the Table of Nations an accurate source of information about the early nations? Give examples.

7. Summarize the significance of Nimrod in earth history.

Chapter 12

The Great Dispersion

Genesis 11:1–32

One of the most amazing phenomena of human history is the strange fact that, despite the essential biological unity of all nations and "races," there are more than 3,000 different languages among men. Each language is significantly different from all others, and it is often true that the more primitive tribes use the more complex languages. All human languages are separated by an essentially infinite barrier from the sounds made by animals, although the vocal organs as such may not be greatly different. The origins of language in general and of languages in particular, are thus inexplicable in terms of evolution, and yet it is impossible to overestimate the importance of articulate, propositional (as distinct from merely reflexive or emotional) speech in the life of mankind. Genesis 11 is the final chapter in Genesis dealing with the nations in general, as distinct from the chosen nation, Israel, and it provides the only true explanation for the origin of languages.

The transition from the dispensation of all nations to the dispensation of the chosen nation resulted from a remarkable series of events in the land of Shinar, only 500 miles south of the Ark still resting on Mount Ararat. There a great city was built and the course of world history was changed.

Much of Biblical history after the Flood can be regarded as a "tale of two cities," — Jerusalem, the "city of peace," and Babylon the "city of confusion." The former is the city in which God has chosen to center His revelation, where He established His temple, and from which one day Christ will reign over all the earth. Spiritually, it is the type of the new Jerusalem, the bride of Christ, — of that "Jerusalem which is above, the mother of us all" (Galatians 4:26). Babylon, on the other hand, is the city where Satan appears to have established the center of *his* kingdom on earth, his base of operations from which to continue and enlarge his rebellion against God. Spiritually, Babylon is the "mother of harlots and abominations of the earth" (Revelation 17:5), the fountain head of all the false religious systems of the world.

Nimrod and the Tower of Babel

After the Flood, the immediate descendants of Noah, of course, all spoke the same language, the same as had been spoken by men in the antediluvian period. It is possible that this was a Semitic language, since the proper names of men and places in the pre-Babel period all have meanings only in Hebrew and its cognate languages.

It had been God's commandment to the sons of Noah that they "be fruitful and multiply and fill the earth" (Genesis 9:1). In order that this might be accomplished in an orderly manner, God had ordained the principle of human government (9:6). This evidently was to be implemented through subdividing the future population into workable and controllable social units or nations. Each organized national group would thus contribute in its own way to the corporate life of mankind as a whole, even as each individual family unit would contribute to its own nation. The diligence with which each would make the contribution of which he was capable would be reflected in the material rewards which would accrue to him and his family as a result. Similarly, those nations which contributed most significantly to the benefit of mankind as a whole would be recognized and rewarded correspondingly. Such recognition and reward is clearly the most effective incentive to diligence and faithfulness in service. This principle seems to be deeply ingrained in human nature and is endorsed by God himself (I Corinthians 3:14; Revelation 22:12).

If any individual or any group should attempt to gain advantage over another by dishonest methods, however, he would be restrained and penalized by the governmental authority established under God for this very purpose. Such a social structure should have been most conducive to the development of a strong sense of both individual and corporate responsibility to God. It also should have encouraged the greatest appreciation of God's grace, which was manifest in His providential maintenance of the physical conditions for life (Genesis 8:21, 22) and His promise of ultimate redemption and salvation.

But, as it turned out, men in general refused to submit willingly to this arrangement, and God had to bring it about by special intervention. As men began to multiply, they preferred to live together in *one* unit, instead of separating into many units. As they migrated from the forbidding region of Ararat, they finally came to the fertile Mesopotamian plain and decided to settle there and build a city. Perhaps they thought that here they might even be able to restore the conditions of Eden itself, for they named the rivers Tigris and Euphrates, after two of the streams that had once flowed from the Garden.

The whole population was said to be originally of "one language and one speech," perhaps a reference to a common spoken language and a common written language. The prevalent opinion that writing was a relatively late development, proceeding through stages of pictographic writing, cuneiform, etc., is generally valid but does not preclude a written language prior to Babel. When the languages were confounded, the nations had to develop a new alphabet and written language to correspond to their new manner of speech. The written tables (the "generations") handed down through the patriarchal line, however, were presumably still in Shem's possession, later to be passed on to Terah and eventually to Moses. It is probable, in fact, that Shem and his immediate family did not participate in the rebellion at Babel and therefore their language was not affected.

It is likely that both Noah and Shem were still living when the Tower of Babel was built, unless there are large gaps in the genealogies, of which we know nothing. If there are no such gaps, Peleg, "in whose days the earth was divided" (Genesis 10:25) was born only 101 years after the Flood, and it seems reasonable that his name (meaning "division") was given him by his father Eber (whose own name is preserved in the term "Hebrew") in commemoration of the great disper-sion. In view of the longevity of early post-diluvian man, and God's intention to "fill the earth," a little calculation will reveal that it would have been quite possible for the earth's population to have grown to several thousand within one hundred years after the Flood.

Assuming Noah and Shem were still living, it is most unlikely that they would have joined in the Babel enterprise, and Japheth also may have remained aloof. Many of their sons and grandsons seem to have participated, however, since they were included among those in the "dividing" of the nations. It is clear though that the Hamites were the most prominent par-ticipants in the rebellion, under the dynamic leadership of Nimrod.

It is probable that Ham and his sons deeply resented Noah's prophecy of the curse on their family. This is intimated in the fact that Cush named one of his sons Nimrod, which means "Let us rebel!" Had God destined them to perpetual servitude to Shem and Japheth and their descendants? Oh, no! They would rule instead! And so Cush, perhaps encouraged by Ham, began to train Nimrod to struggle for the ascendancy among men.

Thus, Nimrod "began to be a mighty one in the earth" (Gen-esis 10:8), and he soon brought all the Hamites, and possibly many of the Semites and Japhethites under his influence and control. They finally settled in the fertile plain of Shinar (a name probably later identified as "Sumer") and began to build a great complex of cities, with "the beginning of his kingdom at Babel."

Thus the progenitors of the nations of the earth were originally united, with a single language and evidently a common purpose. This seems to be the goal of many people today, their hopes for world peace and prosperity centered in the so called "United Nations." But just as this *first* "united nations" served mainly as a union against God, so will the eventual outgrowth of this present amalgamation of peoples be used as a vehicle of opposition to God.

Nimrod was evidently a very talented and powerful individual and "began to be a mighty one in the earth." Genesis 10:9 can be read: "He was a mighty tyrant before (or 'against') Jehovah." He was a "hunter" in the sense that he was implacable in searching out and persuading men to obey his will. He led them to remain together and to build a strong city where they could "make us a name lest we be scattered abroad upon the face of the whole earth" (Genesis 11:4). He may also have won fame as a hunter of the large animals which were proliferating rapidly over the earth during the early decades after the Flood, and which may have become a serious problem to the less-rapidly growing human population.

Their rebellion was climaxed when they planned to erect a great tower "whose top (would be dedicated) unto the heavens." This tower was probably the prototype of the many later "ziggurats" and temple towers built in Babylonia and in countries all over the world. Remains of this tower, or perhaps one which may have been patterned after it, still exist today near the ruins of ancient Babylon. This Babylonian tower, still known by the Arabs as *birs nimroud,* was over seven hundred feet tall when described by the Greek historian Herodotus in about 450 B.C.

It is probable that Nimrod built a temple at its apex with representations of the "host of heaven." It is not unlikely that Satan himself met with him here and instructed him in the secrets of his own rebellion against God, in which Nimrod became a willing ally. After his death, Nimrod was accepted by his followers as the human incarnation of God (or, rather, of the one who *aspired* to be God). His name was preserved as "Merodach," or "Marduk," the chief deity of the Babylonians.

Although the curtain had now been drawn, as it were, on his activities, there can be little doubt that Satan was still energetically working behind the scenes. He pressed his advantage, gained when he capitalized so effectively on the fatal weakness in Ham's character, and soon gained the allegiance of the Hamites in general and Nimrod in particular.

Romans 1:18–32 graphically describes the resulting moral and spiritual deterioration of Nimrod and his followers. Willfully leaving the knowledge and worship of the true God and *Creator,* they began instead to worship the *creation,* and this soon led to pantheism and polytheism and idolatry. How much of this new system of religion came by direct revelation from Satan himself we don't know, but there is abundant evidence that all forms of paganism have come originally from the ancient Babylonian religion. The essential identity of the various gods and goddesses of Rome, of Greece, India, Egypt, and other nations with the original pantheon of the Babylonians is well established.

These pagan deities were also identified with the stars and planets, the "host of heaven," with sun-worship occupying a central place. This system was formalized in the Zodiac, with its numerous constellations — a most remarkable construction which was the common possession of all the nations of antiquity. And behind all this facade of "men and birds and four-footed beasts and creeping things," represented in the stars, lurked a real "host of the heavens," the angelic and demonic hosts of Lucifer, the "day-star." It is possible that the entire system may have been a gross corruption of the true evangelical significance of the heavenly bodies, created originally to serve in part for "signs and seasons," but in any case, as it was interpreted by Nimrod and his followers, it soon led to astrology and spiritism and all the other evils of paganism and idolatry.

It seems likely that the Tower of Babel was built as a great temple, with its top intended to serve as a shrine "unto heaven," probably with the stars and Zodiacal signs emblazoned on its roof and walls, in the manner of other ancient temples. As the center of worship, it would unify the people, "lest they be scattered abroad upon the face of the whole earth," in their opposition to God and His purposes and in their allegiance (perhaps knowingly in the case of Nimrod and other initiates, unknowingly in the cash of most) to Satan and his program.

With tremendous power within their reach as a result of this new occult knowledge and their unity of purpose, God took note that *"nothing"* will now be restrained from them which they have imagined to do (Genesis 11:6). It was time once again for Him to intervene in the affairs of men.

The Confusion of Tongues

The name "Babel" originally seems to have meant "the gate of God," but by a transliteration was identified with the Hebrew word for "confusion" after the tremendous event which took place there. This united rebellion against God was made possible because all men could be brought under the persuasive influence of a single powerful leader. But suddenly they began to discover that, except for immediate members of the family, they could no longer communicate with each other. By some inexplicable and marvelous alteration of those brain centers which store information on the thought-content associated with particular formulations of sound by the vocal chords, God "did there confound the language of all the earth."

When they could no longer communicate, they finally quit building the city and each family unit gradually left the area, migrating into some other part of the world to establish its own "nation." Thus were the original seventy nations listed in Genesis 10, established "after their families, after their tongues, in their lands, after their nations" (Genesis 10:5, 20, 31). These have since proliferated into over 150 major nations and more than 3,000 tongues.

The faculty of human speech and language is truly one of the most amazing attributes of mankind. The fundamental nature of speech in the very identity of man is underscored in the revelation of God to man through His *Word*. Christ Himself is the *living* Word! "God has *spoken* to us in His Son" (Hebrews 1:2). It is not too much to say that this was the very reason man was created able to speak and to hear — in order that there might first be communication between God and man and, secondarily, between man and man. But when men began to prostitute this divine gift in order to cooperate in rebellion against their Maker, God, in a most appropriate judgment, proceeded to "confound their language that they may not understand one another's speech" (Genesis 11:7).

How this miracle was accomplished is not revealed. The various families suddenly found they could no longer communicate with other families and if they couldn't communicate, they couldn't cooperate. Misunderstandings and incoherent arguments surely multiplied rapidly under such conditions, and the only solution finally was for each family to move somewhere else, leaving only King Nimrod and his immediate family to dwell in Babel, in what must have bern a state of bitter frustration for some time to come.

But something about the Hamitic languages introduced by the confusion of tongues seems to impel endless proliferation and variety. Although all can be described roughly as "agglutinative" languages, they are extremely intricate and divergent in their structure. Every little Indian or African tribe seems to have developed its own language, by virtue of its own isolation and the peculiarly concrete and materialistic thought-structure inherent in Hamitic peoples.

As they scattered, they left behind any knowledge of writing they may have possessed and had to begin again to develop a written language to fit their new speech. They took with them at least a partial recollection of the religious system developed by Nimrod, and made this the foundation of their own religion which accounts for the basic similarity of all the religions of the pagan world. At the same time they also carried with them a vague remembrance of the great Flood, and the true God and His promise of a coming Saviour.

The different family units migrated away from Babel until they found suitable areas in which to settle and develop their own respective cultures and civilizations. Those that were the strongest or most intelligent or most industrious no doubt took over the best sites, fairly near to the center of dispersion in Babel, eventually producing the great civilizations that developed in the ancient Middle and Near East (Egypt, Elam, Assyria, Hittites, etc.). Others were forced to settle farther away, thus taking somewhat longer to produce their own civilizations (Greece, India, China, etc.). Gradually, still others migrated to more distant lands, eventually reaching southern and western Africa and even into the Americas. Those tribes that were forced up into northern Europe or into the far interior of Africa had to struggle against harsh environmental conditions—the great ice sheet of the post-Flood glacial period in the one case, and the equatorial rains and heat in the other—and some of them eventually died out. These included such people as the Neanderthals, who once were thought to be primitive ape-men because of their brutish appearance but who are now known to have been true men suffering from the deformations of rickets and arthritis caused by the rigors of the cold dark climates in which they lived.

As each family began its new life in a new and unfamiliar region, they were forced to live simply for many years — mainly by hunting animals and gathering fruits and nuts for food, living in caves or crude wooden shelters, and surviving off the land as best they could, fashioning implements and weapons out of stones and sticks and utensils out of clay. Though they knew the arts of metallurgy and building construction quite well, they first had to find sources of metals and building materials. Similarly, although they knew how to raise crops and domesticate animals, it would take them many years to develop a stable agriculture and productive herds. The problem was complicated by their small numbers, as complex economies require many specialists, a luxury that was impossible when each family member had to devote most of his attention to the problem of survival.

This period of small tribal populations living in a "hunting and gathering" economy, with crude stone implements, is often recognized as the initial stage of culture at each occupation site, but it has been misinterpreted by evolutionary archaeologists as indicating a Paleolithic ("Old Stone Age") period. It would not have taken a million years or more for early man to have emerged from this stage as evolutionists claim, but only a few decades or generations in most cases (actually, of course, there are some tribes living even today who are living in this type of culture).

More and more evidence is being accumulated today that high civilizations developed almost contemporaneously all over the world, in each case after only a brief period of "hunting and gathering" culture in each region. None of these, however, are as old as the very first post-Flood civilizations in the Middle East.

Nimrod himself presumably remained at Babel and, though his following and influence were no longer worldwide, as they had been, he and his descendants still managed to develop a strong nation and civilization there in Shinar. These were the Sumerians, the first inhabitants of Babylon.

God will, in the millennium, "restore to the people a pure language that they may all call upon the name of Jehovah to serve him with one consent" (Zephaniah 3:9), but even then there will be distinct nations (Micah 4:1–5), each fulfilling its intended mission for the earth as a whole. Even in the "new earth" which God will create after the millennium, there will *still* be "nations of them who are saved" walking in the light of God's eternal city (Revelation 21:24).

Thus God definitely has a place for distinct nations, not only in this present world, but in eternity. Until Christ comes, the only "United Nations" or "One World" of which the Scriptures speak is the coming kingdom of the beast (Revelation 13:7, 8; 17:13, 14), which was foreshadowed long ago by Nimrod and his kingdom at Babylon.

God having divided the nations and confused their tongues, one particular nation and language must now be chosen through which He could speak to men, through whom His written Word would be revealed. In accordance with Noah's prophecy, the family of Shem was chosen and the particular genealogical line through Arphaxad, Salah, Eber, Peleg, Reu, Serug, Nahor and Terah was maintained for this purpose. The "generations of Shem" ended with the record of the dispersion at Babel, and the "generations of Terah" (Genesis 11:27) recorded the above genealogy. It fell to Terah's son Abram to give complete obedience to God's command, and to journey all the way to the promised land. Thus, eventually, "to Abraham and his seed were the promises given" (Galatians 3:16).

From this point on in the book of Genesis, as in the Old Testament as a whole, the focus of attention is on this chosen nation, Israel. The first eleven chapters of Genesis, which have been our particular object of study in this book, deal with the primeval history of all mankind. It is this section, of course, which has come under the greatest attack by evolutionists and skeptics of all kinds. Nevertheless, as we have emphasized, these early chapters of Genesis are true and historical in every respect. It is absolutely imperative for us today, if we would really comprehend the modern world and plan effectively for the future world, to understand and believe this divinely-inspired history of the primeval world.

Questions for Discussion

1. What is the evolutionist's explanation of the development of human language from animal noises?

2. Discuss the significance of Babel and Babylon in world history.

3. What significance can you see in the rebuilding of Babylon going on for the past 20 years?

4. Why did God scatter the tribes at Babel and give each tribal or family unit its own distinct language?

5. What is the evidence that evolutionism, pantheism, astrology, spiritism, and idolatry all originated at Babel and then reached all nations?

6. Will the nations of the world ever have a single language again?

7. Discuss the archaeological implications of the small tribes radiating from Babel and having to develop their own separate cultures.

Chapter 13

The World to Come

II Peter 3

The vital importance of the Genesis record — especially of Creation and the Flood — in the context of the imminent return of Christ, is emphasized in the New Testament over and over again. The "last days" were to be characterized by a denial of the "first days," and it would be especially urgent in those days that the preaching of "the *everlasting* gospel" stress worship of God as Creator, the one who "made heaven, and earth, and the sea, and the fountains of waters" (Revelation 14:6, 7). One of the most significant and illuminating chapters in the Bible is the last chapter written by the great Apostle Peter just before his martyrdom.

In the third chapter of II Peter, God has given us a remarkable prophetic foreview of the basic issues in the end-time conflict between Christianity and anti-Christianity, contrasting the world-view of the evolutionist and uniformitarian with the true framework of history as given in the Scriptures. It is appropriate that we conclude our study of Genesis 1–11 with a study of this important New Testament commentary on these subjects.

The World That Then Was (II Peter 3:1–6)

It was Peter's great confession of faith in the Son of God that became the very foundation of the church which Jesus built

(Matthew 16:16–19). He it was whose use of the "keys of the kingdom" first opened the door of the church to both Jews (Acts 2:36–39) and Gentiles (Acts 10:44–48). And now, near the very end of this ministry, God permitted him to look forward in the Spirit to the last days of the church and to prophesy of the conditions which it would then have to meet and overcome.

It is significant that, in the context of the latter-day apostasy which he foretold, Peter repeatedly urged the believers to cling to the Scriptures (1:19–21; 3:16), just as also did Paul in *his* last writing (II Timothy 3:14–4:4). In this third chapter, Peter begins by exhorting his readers to be saturated with both the Old Testament ("words spoken before by the holy prophets") and the New Testament ("words spoken of us the apostles of the Lord and Saviour").

The reason for this warning is that they might be forearmed against the powerful attack of latter-day "scoffers" against the climactic theme of both Testaments, *"the promise of his coming."* Men in the last days (including especially the false teachers in the professing church, described in tragic detail in II Peter 2) would completely reject the sovereign power and righteous judgment of the Creator. They would ridicule the oft-repeated Biblical promise of His coming, His promise to complete His work of redemption and deliverance of a creation that had been groaning in pain ever since man's sin brought God's Curse upon it.

And the philosophical foundation of this denial would be the *principle of uniformity!* "All things continue as they were." In effect, these latter-day religious and educational leaders would be saying: "Our modern mind can no longer accept the naive teachings of the fathers concerning the supernatural intervention of a transcendent God in the uniform course of nature. We no longer need to resort to the concept of miracles, since science has proved the universe always to operate in accord with the laws of chemistry and physics."

One might object that, even if the principle of uniformity prevails at present, it is still necessary to explain the existence of the universe in terms of a divine Creator. "Oh, not so," says the intellectual, "all things continue as they were since the *beginning,* not the end, of creation. Creation was no different from the processes that still continue. Everything has been gradually organized and brought into its present state by means of the same natural laws and processes which exist at present. Thus creation is still going on; however, since science can account for everything and no actual 'creator' is needed, we should call it 'evolution' instead of 'creation.' There has never been a real creation or any other supernatural interruption of these present processes, and therefore it is foolish and reactionary to be concerned about any possible future interruption. Forget about this outdated notion of God coming someday to judge and change the world!"

This of course is exactly and precisely the intellectual attitude prevailing almost universally in the modern world. The pseudo-scientific philosophy of evolutionary uniformitarianism professes to be able to explain the universe and all its inhabitants in terms of natural development under the uniform operation of natural law.

But it should be obvious that modern "science," in the true sense of the word, is able to study only the present cosmos. The antediluvian cosmos is no longer accessible for scientific measurement and observation. Such relics of the first cosmos as may have survived into the present world can of course be studied scientifically in their *present* condition, but this can tell us nothing directly about their former conditions of existence. The only genuine sources of information for an antediluvian cosmology would be either the historical records of eyewitnesses or divine revelation. The Biblical record in Genesis is both.

However, there is an alternative approach which has now become widely accepted, in spite of its inherent fallacies and self-contradictions. This is the famous *principle of uniformitarianism,* first popularized by the British geologist, Sir Charles Lyell, about the middle of the nineteenth century. This is the principle that present physical processes, acting essentially at the same rates as they do now, can explain the origin and development of all the earth's physical and biological phenomena, there is thus no need to postulate any special events of supernatural creation or catastrophic divine intervention in nature. This principle obviously demands great ages of geologic time for the slow development of all the earth's structures, and its tremendous complexity and variety of living things.

Charles Darwin was profoundly influenced by Lyell's theories; the Darwinian theory of evolution by natural selection explicitly requires uniformitarianism and the geologic ages for its foundation. Darwinism in turn has had a most far-reaching influence on almost every field of modern thought. The theoretical structure of all the biological and social sciences has been superposed on the evolutionary framework. The assumed kinship of man with the animals and the supposed evolutionary continuity of nature and history is basic in every form of anti-Christian teaching today. Evolutionism will be found undergirding and permeating communism, fascism and all other varieties of socialism and totalitarianism, as well as practically all religions other than Biblical Christianity.

This evolutionary-uniformitarian framework of earth history of course categorically rejects the concept of a special period of Creation and a subsequent world-destroying Deluge. To this system there is only one cosmology with neither beginning nor end. The promise of a future purgation of the earth by fire and creation of a new cosmos is even more repugnant to this system of thought than is the great Flood.

But the exciting thing about all this is that Peter, in this third chapter, predicted this exact state of affairs as characteristic of the last days! He prophesied that men would mock at the teaching of the coming of the Lord, which had been promised by the holy prophets and fathers since the world began (Acts 3:21)—saying, "All things continue as they were since the *beginning* of the creation" (II Peter 3:4). Note especially that "creation" is, in their view, still continuing, since continuity is assumed not just since the end, but since the *beginning* of the creation! This statement is a wonderfully precise and succinct statement of the modern evolutionary uniformitarian worldview.

But then Peter, with equally precise insight, exposes the utter fallacy of the evolutionary system simply by setting forth the Biblical framework of history. This framework, with reference to the past cosmology, is centered around a real Creation and the Deluge. Implicit also, though not specifically mentioned, are the Fall and Curse, which laid the foundation for events leading finally to the Flood. The evidence for these events is so tremendous, says Peter, and their refutation of uniformitarianism is so devastating, that the evolutionist is nothing less than "willfully ignorant."

According to Peter, the entire history of the world can be divided into three great eras, each identified by its own particular cosmic structure and each separated from the others by a devastating cataclysm. These three eras are identified as follows: (1) "the heavens and the earth which were of old," described in verses 5 and 6; (2) "the heavens and the earth which are now," in verses 7–12; and (3) the "new heavens and a new earth," in verse 13. The first two eras are separated by the Flood, which destroyed the "world (Greek *kosmos*) that then was"; the last two are separated by the coming "day of the Lord," in which the present world will be destroyed by fire (3:10). The organized study of the characteristics of each of the three worlds—that is, each cosmos, the earth and its atmospheric heavens—is called a "cosmology."

The very fact that this is the *Biblical* framework is sufficient evidence of its validity. The Bible is the Word of God, and

God is the Creator. If men reject or ignore this fact, their unbelief does not affect God's truth (Romans 3:3) — it merely exposes their own rebellious hearts.

But, as a matter of fact, this is also the cosmological framework supported by all *true* science, as distinguished from "science falsely so-called" (1 Timothy 6:20). The two laws of thermodynamics (confirmed empirically in thousands of experiments ranging from the sub-nuclear scale to the astronomic scale with no known exceptions), bear strong witness to the fact of a real and finished Creation. The first law, that of energy conservation, demonstrates that creation is *not* occurring at present. The second law, that of energy degradation, demonstrates that the universe is not infinitely old (otherwise the universe would already have completely run down) and therefore had a beginning or *creation!*

Furthermore, the second law, with its implications of disorder, decay, and death in the universe supports the Biblical record of God's Curse on the world. And the greatest physical evidence of the presence of death in the world is found in the very rocks of the earth's crust, containing the fossil remains of innumerable animals that once lived and then died. Instead of being a record of evolutionary history, this worldwide exhibit of judgment and death constitutes the very plainest testimony, for all who are not willfully ignorant, concerning the historical reality of the Curse and the Flood. And this in turn utterly refutes the framework of evolutionary uniformitarianism.

These two great facts of history — special creation in the beginning, and the later worldwide flood — are confirmed by the real facts of science and are offered by Peter as such devastating evidence against the evolutionary uniformitarian cosmology that those who believe in the latter are said to be "*willingly* (and, therefore, *culpably*) ignorant." These facts are also, of course, clearly recorded in Genesis and are referred to in many other parts of the Bible.

The first of these two facts is that there was a real Creation. "The heavens and earth were of old, by the Word of God" (not by uniform evolutionary processes, but "standing" by the Word of God). "By the word of the Lord were the heavens made, and all the host of them by the breath of his mouth. For he spake and it was done; he commanded and it stood fast" (Psalm 33:6, 9). "... (God's) works were *finished* from the foundation of the world" (Hebrews 4:3; see also Genesis 2:1–4; Exodus 20:11).

The second great fact of history of which the latter-day scoffers are willfully ignorant is the great Flood. "Whereby the world that then was, being overflowed with water, perished." Not only is the principle of uniformity inadequate to account for the events of Creation, but it is not even adequate to account for all events *since* the Creation. The "heavens and earth which were of old, standing by the Word of God," were thus destroyed at the time of the Flood.

Consequently, the uniformitarian assumption is valid, at most, only back to the Flood. The Flood constituted a great "discontinuity" in the earth's normal processes. It is therefore impossible to project present rates (whether of sedimentation, radioactivity, erosion, or other geologic processes) into the antediluvian period, and even more so into the Creation period. These processes, as well as most other earth processes, were tremendously enlarged and intensified during the Flood.

As we have noted before, the only significant scientific ev- idence supporting the theory of evolution is the supposed geologic history of life on the earth as preserved in the fossil-bearing rocks of the earth's crust. But these must all be dated subsequent to the Fall and the Curse, since there was no death in the world before then. Furthermore, these fossils must, in most cases, have been buried suddenly and catastrophically or else they never would have been preserved at all. As we saw in Chapter 9, the most probable explanation for most of these rocks and their fossils is that they were laid down during the terrible year of the great Flood. Thus, instead of demonstrating a slow, uniform, evolutionary history of the earth, they speak instead of a tremendous cataclysm of judgment and destruction in which "the world (Greek *kosmos*) that then was, being overflowed with water, perished."

The World That is Now (II Peter 3:7–18)

Thus the original *cosmos* — the earth and its atmospheric heavens — were brought into being by the creative energy of the Word of God, not by the natural processes which now prevail and are controlled by the two laws of thermodynamics. In ways impossible for us to understand in the present economy, the primeval earth was formed out of water, and constituted, so to speak, in a matrix of water. Waters beneath the earth's surface and waters in vapor form above the firmament (atmosphere) enveloped the earth's surface and its inhabitants, sustaining life in all its varieties.

But when the Flood came, these same waters which had protected the earth now destroyed it. These two historical events — Creation and the Flood — completely invalidate the assumption of uniformitarianism and therefore also the theory of evolution. Thus the first cosmos no longer exists.

The Flood thus marks the chronological boundary between the first cosmos and the present cosmos (the word "cosmos" being used here of the world as an orderly and harmonious system at any time, whether past, present or future). Transliterating the Greek, II Peter 3:6 says, "The cosmos that then was, being cataclysmically flooded with water, perished." The phrase "cataclysmically flooded" is the verb form of the noun used in II Peter 2:5 (there translated by "flood"). See Luke 17:27 also. The word is the Greek *kataklusmos,* and means simply "cataclysmic flood." It is used in the New Testament only to refer to the Noachian Deluge. The antediluvian earth, that is, the earth before the Flood, with its geography and geology included, was radically changed.

The antediluvian heavens with their vapor canopy, climate and atmospheric conditions in general were likewise changed by the Flood. This does not mean that the basic laws of nature were changed, but that the rates of geological and other processes were profoundly disturbed and altered.

Now it is highly important to recognize that it is only the present cosmos with which science can deal. Science (that is, "knowledge") is the study of the materials and phenomena which exist in the present world. Scientific observations and measurements cannot be made on entities which no longer exist or which do not yet exist. The scientific method necessarily involves reproducibility of experimental results, and thus science, as such, cannot legitimately make pronouncements about either the prehistoric past or the eschatologic future.

There is no conflict whatever between Christianity and true science. The Christian can study and accept all the data of science with no qualms at all, since true science deals only with "the heavens and the earth which are now." At the same time, he should recognize and insist that any real knowledge (that is, "science") dealing either with the "heavens and the earth which were of *old*" or with the "*new* heavens and the *new* earth," for which we look in connection with the derided "promise of his coming" (II Peter 3:13) must depend, at least for its basic framework, on divine revelation.

The present cosmos, "the heavens and the earth which are now," are being kept in store "by the same word." This seems to be an implicit reference to the basic law of science in the present world, the law of conservation of mass and energy — none is either being created or destroyed.

The marvelous mystery of the relation between matter and energy is resolved only in Jesus Christ Himself, who is now "upholding all things by the word of his power" (Hebrews

1:3). Thus, in the last analysis, we can only come to a real understanding of even the *present* world, when we recognize that even these present processes with which true science deals are dependent for their sustenance on the divine Creator, the Lord Jesus Christ!

After the Flood the earth gradually adjusted itself to new land and sea balances. Geological processes gradually approached their present rates and natural phenomena in general finally became more or less stabilized with their present characteristics. This is the true domain of the study of the present world order — "the heavens and the earth which are now."

This era has already lasted many thousands of years and has witnessed the rise and fall of many great nations and civilizations The post-diluvian cosmos has endured much longer than did the antediluvian cosmos, and through all these millennia, except for occasional localized miracles, the world has continued to operate under essentially continuous and uniform natural laws and processes. In fact, God Himself, after the Flood, said it would be so (Genesis 8:21, 22).

It is the study of these present laws and processes that constitutes the legitimate sphere of true science. Even in this present world, there are many lesser catastrophes that interrupt these uniform rates, and true science must take full cognizance of these, too, in erecting its cosmology.

As long as scientists confine themselves to this proper sphere, there is no conflict with Scripture. The Bible has a great many references to natural phenomena and these will be found in strict agreement with all verified scientific data. But when scientists attempt to project present rates and phenomena into the prehistoric past, on the basis of uniformitarian and evolutionary assumptions, ignoring the Creation and the Flood in so doing, then serious differences of course arise. Conflict is also inevitable when scientists use these assumptions to deny the future day of the Lord and His coming.

The present cosmos will not last forever. God has not forgotten His promise, despite the scoffing of uniformitarian intellectuals. He is longsuffering, but "the day of the Lord *will come.*" For, "... one day is with the Lord as a thousand years." That is, geologic work which seemingly would require a thousand years to accomplish at present rates could be done by God in one day. A world which, on the basis of uniformity, seems to be four or five billion years old may thus actually be only several thousand years old. As noted in an earlier chapter, it was necessary for the world to be created with an appearance of age. The "apparent age," at the time at which the cosmic clock was set when it was first wound up was evidently tremendously large perhaps to emphasize the eternity and transcendence of the Creator. But the "true age" revealed in Scripture is quite small, thus emphasizing the temporality and finitude of the Creation.

We are undoubtedly now living in the "last days." Although God is longsuffering, some day soon "the day of the Lord will come as a thief in the night." By comparison with other Scriptures (for example, I Thessalonians 5:2; II Thessalonians 2:2; Isaiah 2:10–12; Zephaniah 1:14–16; Joel 3:1–14; Revelation 6:15–17, and many others) we know that "the day of the Lord" is a technical phrase referring to the period of time in which God again will intervene directly in the affairs and processes of the cosmos. The phrase refers both to the literal day on which He *begins* thus to work and the total period *during* which He works, including the great tribulation and the millennium (Revelation 20:2–6; note also that "a thousand years is as one day").

At the end of the thousand years, the present cosmos will be destroyed by fire, possibly atomic disintegration (II Peter 3:10–11; Revelation 20:11). And then finally, after the last judgment and separation of Satan and all his followers from God forever in the lake of fire, God will establish the "new heavens and new earth" — the third and final and *eternal* cosmos (II Peter 3:13; Revelation 21:1). In this cosmos, "wherein dwelleth righteousness," the Curse will be removed, the second law of thermodynamics will be repealed, and there will be no more pain or death (Revelation 21:4; 22:3). This cosmos will be no less real than the present cosmos, but it will be a *new* (that is, "renovated," cleansed by fire) earth with its atmospheric heavens.

In view of the tremendous implications of these things, Peter makes several pointed applications. Since God's promise is delayed only so that others may come to repentance, we can "hasten the coming" (3:12) by doing all we can to bring men to Christ. As for the unsaved, they should "account that the longsuffering of our Lord is salvation" and hasten to Christ with no further equivocation or delay!

There is no longer any justification for doubting or scoffing. God has given all men overwhelming evidence, both in Scripture and science, that He created all things and that He still controls all things. He has already demonstrated His sovereign power by the worldwide judgment of the Flood. We can be absolutely sure He will fulfill His promise to return and judge this present world in a global Fire. But then, finally — also "according to His promise" — all who have trusted the Lord Jesus Christ for their eternal forgiveness and salvation can look forward with great hope and joy to an unending "new heavens and a new earth, wherein dwelleth righteousness."

Questions for Discussion

1. Why is it appropriate to include a study of II Peter 3 with a study of the early chapters of Genesis?

2. Compare and contrast the three "cosmologies" mentioned in II Peter 3, and the periods of history corresponding to each.

3. Define uniformitarianism and its significance as a scientific premise in geology and other sciences.

4. How is evolutionism predicted in II Peter 3?

5. What does Peter prescribe as the antidote for evolutionary uniformitarianism?

6. Outline the main scientific evidences for special creation and the worldwide flood.

7. What is the real significance of Peter's caution that "one day is with the Lord as a thousand years"?

More on the Subject

This book is essentially an introductory treatment of a vast and fascinating complex of studies. For more thorough treatment of various Biblical and scientific topics covered in Genesis 1–11, the following books by the writer may also be consulted. All have been widely used and recommended by reviewers.

The Genesis Record (Grand Rapids, Baker Book House, 1976), 716 pp., cloth

A complete commentary on the entire book of Genesis, written in easily followed narrative style, but treating in depth all the problem passages. Scientific in treatment, yet Biblical and devotional in application. This quarterly is, to some degree, a condensation of the commentary on Genesis 1 — 11 in *The Genesis Record*. Includes an annotated bibliography on other important commentaries on the book of Genesis.

Scientific Creationism (San Diego, Master Books, 1980), 281pp., paper

A reference handbook on all of the major scientific aspects of the creation-evolution question, plus one chapter discussing in detail the Biblical doctrine of creation and the various theories that have been proposed to harmonize evolution and its geological-ages framework with Genesis. Well-documented and authoritative; includes an extensive reference bibliography of works on scientific and Biblical creationism.

The Genesis Flood (Co-author, John C. Whitcomb, Philadelphia, Presbyterian and Reformed Publishing Co., 1961), 518 pp.

The most comprehensive and most thoroughly documented scientific exposition of the Genesis record of creation and the flood, providing an effective system for unifying and correlating scientific and Biblical data bearing on the earth's early history. Thorough treatment of the geologic and geochronometric data, with reinterpretation in terms of recent creationism and catastrophism.

The Long War against God (Grand Rapids, Baker Book House, 1989), 344 pp., cloth

The most extensive analysis in print of the age-long reign and worldwide devastating influence of evolutionism, which, in various forms, has been the most basic and deadly weapon of Satan in his long warfare against the Creator. Thoroughly and compellingly documented, with full indexes of topics, authors and Scriptures.

The Biblical Basis for Modern Science (Grand Rapids, Baker Book House, 1986), 516 pp., cloth

The most comprehensive text/reference book on all aspects of modern science in relation to Scripture. Chapter on each field of science and its harmony with the Bible, plus special chapters on miracles, theology, etc. Many illustrations, appendices and indexes.

The Remarkable Record of Job (Grand Rapids, Baker Book House, 1988), 146 pp., cloth

A unique exposition of the fascinating book of Job, showing its contemporaneity with Genesis. Many important insights on modern science, as well as references to creation, the flood, the dispersion and other events of primeval history — including dinosaurs, cave men, etc.

Science and the Bible (Chicago, Moody Press, 1986), 154 pp., paper

An easy-to-understand exposition of the scientific, historical, prophetic and logical evidences for the inerrant divine truth and authority of Scripture.

The Revelation Record (Wheaton, Tyndale Publishing House, 1983), 521 pp., cloth

A verse-by-verse literal commentary on the Bible's prophetic book of the last days, showing the fulfillment of God's purposes in creation. Scientific and realistic, as well as devotional and Christ-centered throughout.